PARIS HILTON

PARIS HILTON

A Biography

Sandra Gurvis

GREENWOOD BIOGRAPHIES

 GREENWOOD

AN IMPRINT OF ABC-CLIO, LLC
Santa Barbara, California • Denver, Colorado • Oxford, England

Library of Congress Cataloging-in-Publication Data

Gurvis, Sandra.
  Paris Hilton : a biography / Sandra Gurvis.
    p. cm. — (Greenwood biographies)
  Includes bibliographical references and index.
  ISBN 978-0-313-37940-6 (alk. paper) — ISBN 978-0-313-37941-3 (ebook)
1. Hilton, Paris, 1981– 2. Celebrities—United States—
Biography.   3. Socialites—United States—
Biography.   I. Title.
  CT275.H59926G87   2011
  973.931'092—dc22
  [B]   2010041003

ISBN: 978-0-313-37940-6
EISBN: 978-0-313-37941-3

15 14 13 12 11   1 2 3 4 5

This book is also available on the World Wide Web as an eBook.
Visit www.abc-clio.com for details.

Greenwood
An Imprint of ABC-CLIO, LLC

ABC-CLIO, LLC
130 Cremona Drive, P.O. Box 1911
Santa Barbara, California 93116-1911

This book is printed on acid-free paper ∞

Manufactured in the United States of America

For my daughter Amy, fashionista
and creative soul extraordinaire

CONTENTS

SERIES FOREWORD

In response to high school and public library needs, Greenwood developed this distinguished series of full-length biographies specifically for student use. Prepared by field experts and professionals, these engaging biographies are tailored for high school students who need challenging yet accessible biographies. Ideal for secondary school assignments, the length, format, and subject areas are designed to meet educators' requirements and students' interests.

Greenwood offers an extensive selection of biographies spanning all curriculum-related subject areas including social studies, the sciences, literature and the arts, history and politics, as well as popular culture, covering public figures and famous personalities from all time periods and backgrounds, both historic and contemporary, who have made an impact on American and/or world culture. Greenwood biographies were chosen based on comprehensive feedback from librarians and educators. Consideration was given to both curriculum relevance and inherent interest. The result is an intriguing mix of the well known and the unexpected, the saints and sinners from long-ago history and contemporary pop culture. Readers will find a wide array of subject choices from fascinating crime figures like Al Capone to inspiring pioneers like Margaret Mead, from the greatest minds of our time like Stephen Hawking to the most amazing success stories of our day like J. K. Rowling.

While the emphasis is on fact, not glorification, the books are meant to be fun to read. Each volume provides in-depth information about the subject's life from birth through childhood, the teen years, and adulthood. A thorough account relates family background and education, traces personal and professional influences, and explores struggles, accomplishments, and contributions. A timeline highlights the most significant life events against a historical perspective. Bibliographies supplement the reference value of each volume.

INTRODUCTION

"That's hot." The tall, thin blonde sits in the guest chair of *The Late Show with David Letterman,* tosses her long, artfully streaked hair, and crosses her endless legs encased in a designer micromini, revealing just enough thigh to offset that childlike voice with a touch of vixen. This is the image most of America still conjures up for Paris Hilton—very rich, very dumb, and very blonde. She was the one in the sex video, and the one who got thrown in jail for drunken driving, although technically the charges were for violating the terms of her probation. Most people have a difficult time understanding why Paris Hilton remains in the limelight and just shrug her off as an heirhead who is simply famous for being famous.

It's easy to dismiss Paris as someone who's been lucky or always in the right place at the right time. Even those who think they know her have made that assumption. Shortly before she died at age 30 in January 2010 from complications from diabetes and self-neglect, fellow heiress Casey Johnson of the Johnson & Johnson fortune expressed envy of her childhood friend's success: Although "I love [Paris] . . . I hate that she has everything and everything has gone her way."[1] Like many people, she neglected to consider how hard Paris worked at her various undertakings, not to mention the many stumbling blocks and critics she encountered on her way to fame and fortune.

Paris Whitney Hilton was born in New York City on February 17, 1981. The scion of the rich and powerful Hilton family, her paternal great-grandfather was hotelier and industrial magnate Conrad "Connie" N. Hilton, who started with $5,000 in 1919 and parlayed it into a mega-hotel chain worth $165 million at the time of his death in 1979. His son Barron, Paris's grandfather and father of her dad Rick, has been listed in the Forbes 400 richest Americans as having assets of approximately $2.3 billion, while Rick himself is estimated to be worth a mere $300 million, thanks to real estate and other investments. While her mom, Kathy Richards Hilton's, side of the family was considered middle to upper-middle class, they did have inroads into show business, thanks to her unabashedly ambitious and by some accounts ruthless maternal grandmother, Kathleen Mary Dugan Avanzino Richards Catain Fenton. "Big Kathy," as she was known—Paris's mom was "Little Kathy"—pushed all three of her daughters into show business and into marrying rich, with varying degrees of success.

So if she wanted to, Paris could have never worked a single day in her life. She could have simply sat back and been a debutante, joined the country club and played tennis and golf, and married equally wealthy, ensuring a lifetime of security and luxury. Or she could have gone wild, spending her parents' money, overindulging in drugs and alcohol, and travelling the world aimlessly, looking for the next new thrill. Yet she chose the difficult path of public exposure, subjecting herself and her family to all sorts of criticism and ridicule, much of it unfair but in some cases well-founded.

From the time she and her younger sister Nicky became the phenomenon of "the Hilton Sisters," attending club openings and other social gatherings in New York City at the turn of this century, Paris had a strong sense of self. "There is no sin in life worse than being boring—and nothing worse than letting other people tell you what to do," she has said.[2] And indeed Paris has been anything but—graduating from trendy club kid to model to TV and movie personality and finally to entrepreneur. She has moved past being part of a duo, first with her sister Nicky, with whom she still maintains a close and loving relationship, and then with childhood pal Nicole Richie, the latter being her best friend forever (BFF) and then "frenemie" and then back again as part of *The Simple Life* TV show. Paris went on to forge a new franchise on reality TV, the popular and award-winning BFF series. She recorded an album and wrote two books, also with success. And she's reaping in millions with a variety of Paris Hilton product lines, from sunglasses to perfumes to watches to lingerie. In other words, she's become a "brand." "I'm always working. Even if I go somewhere for fun, I end up having to work."[3] Not that she minds, because it has paid off big and she loves what she does.

But Paris has failed spectacularly as well. First with Rick Salomon, an early boyfriend whom, depending upon which account the reader wishes to believe, she allowed to tape their most intimate moments. As soon as Paris became famous, the "1 Night in Paris" video not surprisingly showed up on the Internet and later as a DVD. Then she flagrantly ignored repeated warnings that her driver's license had been suspended and disregarded the conditions of her probation—and ended up in jail for 23 days, a situation that could have easily been avoided had she followed the rules.

But then, Paris was never one to color inside the lines. Just ask her family, who supported her early attempts at selling cookies and toys or the chums from the seven high schools she attended (and whether she actually received a GED has never been officially confirmed). The half-nude photo of her making a rude gesture in a 2000 *Vanity Fair* article presents a perfect portrait of teenaged defiance. She's always been game to try new things—whether it's falling off a horse and injuring herself while filming *The Simple Life* or setting herself up as a politically incorrect sex goddess in *The Hottie and the Nottie*, what many consider to be one of the worst movies ever made. She's taken it in the chin, from both critics and friends—and people she thought at the time she could trust—and while she's admitted that some of what has been said has deeply hurt her, she keeps moving forward. She's not afraid to laugh at herself, whether its falling into a blossom-covered pond at a Hollywood party while chatting on the phone (she thought the flowers were decorations for the floor) or referring to herself as "annoying" while going undercover as a gas-station attendant on the *I Get That a Lot* TV show.

Her sense of humor and love of living things—particularly small dogs or other animals that resemble them—have helped counter many of the difficult times. While she has said that she takes her dog Tinkerbell, her work, and her family seriously and herself not so much, it is apparent that she has been listening all along and paying close attention to what works for her. "Even when she's using that cooey little baby voice, you can see the wheels turning in her head," social critic and author Michael Musto has remarked.[4]

Indeed, Paris Hilton is a sensitive, bright, and yes, compassionate young woman. She knows she's beautiful and capitalizes on it, and she's brave enough to remain on her own until she finds the right man rather than settle for second best. She works hard at everything and has made lots of mistakes. She will continue to expand her empire, trying new things, whether it's a cleavage-enhancing bra as an alternative to potentially dangerous plastic surgery or incorrectly identifying a leopard as a tiger while on safari in Africa. So, while the rich may be very different, especially considering the current economy, this biography will show that, with Paris Hilton, she's a lot more like you and me than appears on the surface.

NOTES

1. Ani Esmailian, "Casey Johnson Was Jealous of Paris Hilton" (January 13, 2010), www.hollyscoop.com/casey-johnson/casey-johnson-was-jealous-of-paris-hilton_22728.aspx#ixzz0mJFPTwbH.

2. Paris Hilton with Merle Ginsberg, *Confessions of an Heiress* (New York: Fireside, 2005), 5.

3. "Paris, Not France," directed by Adria Petty, Documentary (New York: MTV, 2008), unpublished transcript.

4. Ibid.

TIMELINE: EVENTS IN THE LIFE OF PARIS HILTON

February 17, 1981	Paris Whitney Hilton is born in New York City.
October 5, 1983	Paris's younger sister and lifelong BFF, Nicholai Olivia "Nicky," is born.
1987–89	The Hilton family transitions and makes a permanent move to Los Angeles.
March 26, 1987	Paris makes an early public appearance at the Sixth Annual Celebrity Mother–Daughter Fashion Show in Beverly Hills with mom Kathy, dad Rick, and sister Nicky.
November 7, 1989	Barron Nicholas Hilton II, the third Hilton sibling, is born.
1992 (released July 1993)	Paris's first movie appearance (uncredited) in *Wishman*.
March 3, 1994	Paris's youngest brother, Conrad Hughes Hilton III, is born.
June 1995	Graduates from St. Paul the Apostle grade school in LA.

September 1995 Starts Marymount High School in Bel Air, CA.

1996 Supposedly loses her virginity to Randy Spelling, son of the late legendary TV producer Aaron Spelling and brother of actress and reality-TV star Tori.

Hilton family moves back to NYC and lives at Waldorf-Astoria.

Enrolls briefly at the Convent of the Sacred Heart in NYC.

Enrolls in Professional Children's School (PCS) in NYC.

1997 Transfers to exclusive Dwight School, located in Central Park West.

Begins hitting the club and fashionista circuit with younger sister Nicky, catching the eye of the *New York Post* Page Six gossip columnist and other editors.

November 3, 1997 One of the first official public appearances of the phenomenon known as "The Hilton sisters" at the party for Girls Rule and Bridge Fund in New York City.

1997–98 Tagged as first "celebutante" by *New York Post* Page Six gossip columnist Richard Johnson.

1999 Leaves Dwight unexpectedly, allegedly to spend time at the London Hilton.

Attends Canterbury School in Connecticut for a few months.

Goes to California to stay with grandmother "Big Kathy."

Attends Buckley School in Sherman Oaks, CA.

Attends Palm Valley School in Rancho Mirage, CA.

1999–2000 Is homeschooled and, according to some sources, earns her GED from the Dwight School.

1999–2001 Becomes involved with Rick Salomon, who eventually publishes and distributes the infamous "1 Night in Paris" sex videotape.

September 2000 Seminal article "Hip Hop Debs" is published in *Vanity Fair* magazine, raising the awareness of the Hilton sisters to a national level.

2000 Signs with Donald Trump's T Management modeling agency.

Appears in *Sweetie Pie,* an independently produced thriller about overprivileged teenagers in LA.

2001 Is christened "New York's Leading 'IT' Girl."

2002 Appears in the movie *Nine Lives,* winning some critical praise.

February 17, 2002 Turns 21 and parties in five cities over a 24-hour period—New York, LA, Tokyo, London, and Las Vegas.

Mid-2002–early 2003 First engagement, to fashion model Jason Shaw.

October 2002 Purchases "Tink" aka Tinkerbell, her beloved Chihuahua, from Texas Teacups.

December 2, 2003 *The Simple Life,* her reality TV show with BFF Nicole Richie, premieres to major ratings and runs for five seasons.

December 2003 A shorter version of the "1 Night in Paris" sex video is leaked onto the Internet and immediately becomes viral, resulting in major and, according to Paris, much unwanted publicity and humiliation.

2003–2004   Is involved in a relationship with singer Nick Carter.

2004   Mario Lavandeira, a 28-year-old unemployed Cuban American gay man, decides to rename himself Perez Hilton in honor of his friend Paris and starts PerezHilton.com, one of the most successful gossip blogs to date.

May 2004   Publishes *Confessions of an Heiress: A Tongue-in-Chic Peek Behind the Pose* from Fireside Press, cowritten with Merle Ginsberg, which becomes a *New York Times* bestseller.

June 15, 2004   A 60-minute version of the "1 Night in Paris" Rick Salomon sex tape is released on DVD by Red Light District Video.

August 2004   Tinkerbell is "kidnapped" for six days and then reappears under mysterious circumstances. A publicity stunt is suspected (see below).

September 2004   Tinkerbell "authors" a memoir with D. Resin, *The Tinkerbell Hilton Diaries: My Life Tailing Paris Hilton.*

Is named one of the "10 Most Fascinating People" in the Barbara Walters TV special.

2004–2005   Paris and Nicky are the subjects of an *E! True Hollywood Story* (THS) documentary on trust-fund babies (2004) and a year later on themselves exclusively.

April 2005   Cuts ties with *Simple Life* costar Nicole Richie, refusing to divulge the reason for the split.

May 2005   Melts hearts and skin as Paige Edwards in the thriller *House of Wax*, a remake of the classic 1953 Vincent Price movie, and wins a Teen Choice Award for best movie scream scene.

May–November 2005 Is briefly engaged to another Paris— Greek shipping heir Paris Latsis.

November 2005 Publishes *Your Heiress Diary: Confess It All to Me* from Fireside Press, cowritten with Merle Ginsberg.

Late 2005–May 2006 Dates another Greek shipping heir, Stavros Niarchos III.

August 22, 2006 Releases first album, *Paris*, under the Heiress/Warner Bros. label. The album reaches number six on the Billboard 200 for a week, with the first single, "Stars Are Blind," a Top 10 hit in 17 countries.

August 2006 British graffiti artist Banksy and a music producer known as "Danger Mouse" wage guerrilla warfare on Paris's debut album, replacing some 500 copies of it in British music stores with an altered mockery.

2006 Is voted the second-worst celebrity role model of 2006, behind Britney Spears in a poll conducted by the Associated Press and AOL.

December, 2006 Plays the lead part and is executive producer of *National Lampoon's Pledge This!* a straight-to-DVD film about a goofy sorority in which Paris plays the snobbish president.

September 7, 2006 Is pulled over by officers of the Los Angeles police department (LAPD) for reckless operation of her Mercedes.

September 2006 "Officially" reconciles with Nicole Richie at a public meeting at the Beverly Hills Hotel, although they had actually made up several weeks earlier.

November 2006   Because of the driving charge, Paris's license is suspended from November until the following March.

December 2006   Is pulled over for making an illegal turn and warned that her license is invalid.

January 2007   Pleads no contest to a reckless driving charge, with a penalty of 36 months probation and fines of about $1,500. She is also required to enroll in an alcohol education program by Feb. 12 of that year.

January 15, 2007   Is pulled over again by California Highway Patrol (CHP) officers who inform her that she was driving on a suspended license. She signs a document acknowledging that she was not supposed to drive, putting her copy of the papers in her glove compartment.

February 27, 2007   Is pulled over a third time, this time by Los Angeles County sheriff's deputies, for driving 70 mph in a 35 mph zone with her headlights off.

May 4, 2007   Is sentenced to 45 days at the Century Regional Detention Facility (CRDF), an all-female prison in Lynwood, CA, by Judge Michael Sauer for violating the terms of her probation. She is told to report to the jail by June 5, 2007.

June 3, 2007   Makes a highly visible appearance at the MTV Awards and then turns herself over to the LA County jail to serve her sentence.

June 7, 2007   Is released from the CRDF due to an unspecified medical condition and is to serve the rest of her full sentence (40 days) under home confinement with an electronic monitoring advice.

June 7, 2007	Judge Sauer demands that Paris return to court the next day.
June 8, 2007	Sauer upholds the original 45-day sentence and Paris is sent back to jail to serve the state-mandated 23 days.
June 26, 2007	Is released from CRDF.
June 27, 2007	Goes on *Larry King Live* and announces that she has found God and new meaning in her life.
July 30, 2007	E! announces that *The Simple Life* will not be renewed for a sixth season.
July 2007	Announces that she is working on a new, as-yet-untitled album.
2007	Is designated as the most overrated celebrity by the *Guinness Book of World Records*.
January–November 2008	Becomes involved with Good Charlotte guitarist Benji Madden, whose twin brother Joel is Nicole Richie's significant other and the father of Nicole's two children.
2008	Stars in and is executive producer of *The Hottie and the Nottie* about a geeky guy who has a fantasy crush on his grade school girlfriend. The movie is considered one of the worst ever made by several sources.
September 30, 2008	Season one of the *My New BFF* TV show premieres on MTV and is a ratings success, spawning season two and BFF shows in London and (as yet unaired) in Dubai.
Summer/Fall 2008	Appears in a "Funny or Die" video to refute a comment made about her by presidential candidate John McCain. Clad in a leopard-print swimsuit and heels, she provides a reasoned and rational

compromise for the U.S. energy crisis. The video goes viral with seven million hits and spawns a sequel with actor Martin Sheen of *The West Wing* TV series.

February 2009–April 2010   Ends her on-again, off-again romance with *The Hills* TV show star Doug Reinhardt. As of this writing, she remains single.

2009   The new edition of the *Oxford Dictionary of Quotations* includes the Paris saying, "Dress cute wherever you go, life is too short to blend in."

Wins several awards and nominations for *My New BFF*, including nominations for the Teen Choice Awards for female Choice Reality/Variety TV Star and the show itself as Choice TV Show—Reality/Variety and a Fox Reality Award for "Innovator of Reality TV/ Awards Shows/Special Appearances."

Early 2010   Racy ad for Devassa beer featuring Paris is "banned" in Brazil.

Spring/Summer 2010   Along with a new fragrance "Tease" added to her highly successful perfume line, Paris launches a line of body-flattering lingerie for young women, a safe alternative to plastic surgery.

August 27, 2010   Arrested with current boyfriend Cy Waits for cocaine possession, when a small amount falls out of her purse. Claims that the purse belonged to a friend.

October 27, 2010   Scheduled to appear in court in Las Vegas for felony possession of cocaine.

Chapter 1

A "STAR" IS BORN

Paris Whitney Hilton was born on February 17, 1981, at a New York City hospital to Kathy Avanzino Richards Hilton and Richard "Rick" Hilton, one of several heirs to the Hilton hotel dynasty. The first of four children, "Star," as she was called from day one, was christened at St. Patrick's Cathedral on Fifth Avenue and spent her first few months lolling about in a luxurious penthouse at 220 East Sixty-Seventh Street.

What might seem like the ordinary birth of a run-of-the-mill heiress—if one can so label "trustifundians" aka trust-fund babies—had as its backdrop a wild and woolly roller coaster of family history. This gene pool resulted in the confounding yet dazzling contradiction that is Paris Hilton—a successful businesswoman who heads up a multimillion-dollar entertainment and fashion conglomerate; a serial shopper and former convicted drunk driver who jets off to Japan, London, and Dubai on a whim; a sexy yet vulnerable woman-child who flits from one tumultuous romance to another and searches on reality TV for that perfect BFF (best friend forever).

Her roots, which can illuminate her true colors, hair and otherwise, include her paternal great-great-grandfather, hotelier and industrial magnate Conrad "Connie" N. Hilton (1887–1979) and her lesser-known but perhaps even more ruthless maternal grandmother, Kathleen Mary Dugan Avanzino Richards Catain Fenton (1938–2002). "Big Kathy" was married four times, twice to mobster Jack Catain, and her oldest daughter and Paris's mother was, not surprisingly, called "Little Kathy." Conrad Hilton himself was wed three times, most notably for four years to actress Zsa Zsa Gabor, and his oldest son, playboy and addict Conrad N. ("Nicky") Hilton (1926–69), also had a brief, turbulent, and highly publicized first marriage to a then-teenaged Elizabeth Taylor. In contrast to what often appears in the media, and even in Paris's own published diary, *Confessions of an Heiress*, it is Conrad's second son, William "Barron" Hilton, who is actually Paris's paternal grandfather.[1]

DAD'S SIDE: MINTING HOTEL MONEY

Born into a Catholic family on Christmas Day in the rough-and-ready New Mexico (later Texas) frontier town of San Antonio, Conrad himself was an oldest child of eight siblings. His mother, the former Mary Laufersweiler, instilled strict religious values and made sure he had the proper schooling and upbringing, while his first-generation immigrant Norwegian father, Augustus "Gus" Hilton, ran a family store, A. H. Hilton, which Conrad worked in from childhood. Gus also loaned money, had a livery stable, and eventually purchased a coal mine, which made him one of the richest men in that part of the country.

Connie was a restless soul. "I was twenty-three years old [and] had been working for eleven years," he wrote in his memoir, *Be My Guest*. "So far I had earned a partnership in a store in the town in which I was born. But it was my father's store. A. H. Hilton & Son. A. H. Hilton & Shadow? a small voice within me was questioning. Wasn't it time I formulated a dream of my own?"[2]

So he tried his hand at politics, and with the help of a graveyard vote ("the best people in the county")—his opponent allegedly obtained ballots representing a herd of sheep—was elected, at age 24, to New Mexico's state legislature.[3] The Hiltons have been and remain conservative Republicans, along with being—or claiming to be—staunch Catholics.

But local corruption, graft, and self-interest proved to be too much even for a budding magnate, and he decided to follow the money instead of seeking re-election. In 1913 he opened the New Mexico State Bank of San Antonio. Although the bank initially almost went bust due to dishonest stockholders, Connie was able to pull together enough money to make it a success, at least until he enlisted as an officer in the army when World War I broke out four years later. By the time he came home in 1919, he had $5,000 in savings, which back in those days was a tidy sum.

His father had passed away during the war, so Connie went prospecting for opportunities in the booming, bustling oil town of Cisco, Texas, with the idea of purchasing another bank. Instead he happened upon the Mobley Hotel "a cross between a flophouse and a gold mine," a two-story red-brick structure that did a land-office business, often turning rooms over three times every 24 hours.[4] After borrowing another $45,000 from family and friends, he purchased the Mobley, transforming it into a marvel of efficiency. He replaced the adjacent greasy spoon restaurant with more beds, reduced the size of the front desk, and added a newsstand.[5] Hilton established a "code for success," which was to be the benchmark of all his hotels:

1. Find your own particular talent.
2. Be big.
3. Be honest.
4. Live with enthusiasm.
5. Don't let your possessions possess you.
6. Don't worry about your problems.
7. Look up to people when you can—down to no one.
8. Don't cling to the past.
9. Assume your full share of responsibility in the world.
10. Pray consistently and confidently.[6]

A 21st-century version of this list would appear in great-granddaughter Paris's *Confessions of an Heiress,* although somehow "Always have a tan," "Never drink diet soda," and "If you're happy, wear pink" don't quite have the same emotional impact.[7]

Connie's emphasis on making the best use of space, providing ex-
cellent service, and motivating staff formed the basis of what was to
become a multibillion-dollar, international corporation, with over 500
hotels worldwide, including his third acquisition and first "name" hotel, the Dallas Hilton in 1925, the start of the franchise, and the big
fish, the Waldorf-Astoria in 1949, where Paris would spend some of her
formative years. In between, he acquired the Plaza and the Roosevelt,
also in New York City, Chicago's famed Palmer House, the Sir Francis
Drake in San Francisco, and many other famous landmarks. After the
Great Depression ended in the late 1930s and early '40s, he also built
dozens of Hiltons in Texas, California, New Mexico, and throughout
the nation. All this from a single dusty fleabag in the middle of Nowhere, Texas; no wonder Conrad caused a ruckus among the so-called
establishment as he quickly acquired one "jewel" after another.

Conrad's female conquests were equally impressive and numerous,
although he remained a bachelor until he was 38, considered pretty
unusual during those days. But when he met 18-year-old Mary Ade-
laide Barron of Owensboro, Kentucky, he knew—or at least thought—
he'd found his soul mate. However, she had little formal education and
"hailed from the Kentucky backwoods . . . liked her moonshine, loved
to gamble . . . savored telling dirty jokes and came from what today
might be described as trailer park trash," writes Hilton biographer Jerry
Oppenheimer.[8] Yet in spite of the fact that Mary would soon be leaving "the simple life" for the lap of luxury, "the family wasn't too happy
about it because Mr. Hilton was so much older," Mary's first cousin
Jarred Barron told Oppenheimer.[9] The marriage only lasted nine years
(1925–34) and ended in divorce, producing three children: Conrad Jr.,
aka Nicky; Paris's grandfather Barron in 1927; and Eric Michael Hilton
in 1933.

Also uncommon for the times, Conrad obtained custody of his two
oldest sons while Eric lived with Mary and her new husband, former
football star and coach Mack Saxon. Both Mary and Mack were heavy
drinkers, and while Nick and Barron went to the best schools and
lived in opulent homes, Eric was relegated to barracks-type housing
in Virginia provided to Mack due to his position working in the navy's
physical training program at the Pentagon. Eric was 16 when his stepfather passed away, leaving him alone with an alcoholic mother who

could barely remember to buy groceries. Not that the two older boys had much access to their busy father; Mary's mother, Mayme Barron, moved to Dallas to care for them. However, eventually all three brothers would return to the fold and make their fortunes—in Nicky's case, misfortunes—in the hotel business.

Conrad wed twice after that. In 1942, he took a second wife, Hungarian bombshell Zsa Zsa Gabor. They divorced four years later over charges (hers) of neglect and emotional abuse, including Conrad's notorious thriftiness, which would become an MO throughout generations of Hiltons—earn your own darned money! Zsa Zsa also began a torrid affair with her handsome teenaged stepson, Nicky, who in today's parlance was considered "hot" (or as Paris might say when considering the circumstances, "Eeeuuuw!"). Like Mary Barron Hilton before her, Zsa Zsa received a relative pittance for her divorce settlement and has famously quoted "Conrad Hilton was very generous to me. . . . He gave me 5000 Gideon Bibles." She also claimed that he provided her with one more thing after they split—a daughter, Constance Francesca Hilton, born in 1947. The circumstances of the conception are disputed— Zsa Zsa asserted that she was forced into it while at the Plaza Hotel while Connie denied paternity altogether.

Connie married a third time, in 1976, to Mary Francis Kelly. A longtime family friend, she was, like his mother, a devout Catholic, and a spry 61 to his 88. She remained with him until his death in 1979, at age 91, of pneumonia.

BARRON VS. NICKY

Nicky and Barron Hilton were as different as two brothers could possibly be. Although flashy Nicky has sometimes been credited as being Paris's grandfather, that honor actually goes to the more conservative, low-key Barron, whose brains helped make Hilton International into the $6.2 billion empire it is today.

Nicky's travails were widely chronicled in the 1950s, particularly after he married and almost as quickly divorced Elizabeth Taylor in 1950–51. Along with being a handsome playboy and eligible bachelor around Hollywood, Nicky also developed a reputation as a boozer and a brawler, even hauling off and slugging Barron during a family get-together. Then he'd become remorseful and stop drinking for a time. But something would set him off and he'd start up again. "He'd get physically violent," another actress and former girlfriend Betsy von Furstenberg recalled. "He was just destined to have this terrible, tragic life."[10] Nick also became hooked on the addictive barbiturate Seconal, which was supplied by a family physician friend, a "Dr. Feelgood" who purportedly handed out uppers and downers to family and friends during junkets as various Hilton hotels opened around the world.[11]

Many of Nick's problems stemmed from low self-esteem. According to "BFF" and Maxwell House coffee heir Bob Neal, Nick believed that Connie and Barron looked down on him, especially when it came to the family business. "Nick got squashed all the time and he blamed it on Barron," states Neal. "But the old man was behind everything like that. It wasn't Barron who instituted things. Everything had to have [Connie's] clearance . . . he held the purse strings."[12]

But not in one important instance. Although he gave up active management of the company in 1966 when Barron was named president, Connie remained chairman of the board and continued to work six days a week. Nick, married a second time, to Oklahoma oil heiress Patricia "Trish" McClintock, had been in put in charge of Hilton International, the overseas operation, which Connie also stayed closely involved with. In a case of money being thicker than water, Trans-World Airlines (TWA) made a lucrative bid for Hilton International to Barron and Connie while Nick and his wife were on vacation. "Barron convinced Connie to make the deal, and Connie just listened to Barron," said Trish.

Although Nick lobbied against the deal to the board of directors, "when it came right down to it, the board voted with Conrad. Barron sold out his brother. Nick absolutely was crushed,"[13] she continued. Nick's resulting downward spiral into alcohol and drugs and his pending divorce as a result of his addiction ended with his death in 1969, the cause of which was subject to speculation. Some sources reported cardiac arrest, while others stated it was an overdose.

Fortunately, this scene has yet to replay itself with Barron's grand-daughters, Paris and Nicky. "I was never jealous of Nicky after she was born," Paris writes in *Confessions of an Heiress*. "I was happy to have someone close. So many of my friends were only children."[14] Although,

Paris claims, they do fight sometimes like normal sisters, the two don't compete; if they like the same outfit, they each purchase one. Although most siblings can hardly afford that type of conflict resolution, even in matters of the heart, "she's the one girl I trust with my boyfriends, no matter what. Our bond is stronger than any bond either of us could have with a guy."[15]

Except for his business deals, which have been widely documented, Barron's life is as private as his brother's was public. Although he initially rebelled against the family business by turning down a $160 per month management position, he changed his mind after a stint as a WWII navy photographer in Hawaii. It was during this time that he became fascinated by aviation and attended the University of Southern California Aeronautical School, receiving his pilot's license, a lifelong passion that culminated in the 750,000-acre Flying-M Ranch in Nevada, from where in 2007 adventurer Steve Fossett took off and never returned.

In 1947, Barron married and remained wed to Marilyn June Hawley (1928–2004), a contractor's daughter from Los Angeles. In keeping with the spirit of Catholicism, the union was fruitful and bore eight children: William Barron Hilton Jr. (born 1948); Hawley Anne Hilton (born 1949); Stephen Michael Hilton (born 1950); David Alan Hilton (born 1952); Sharon Constance Hilton (born 1953); Daniel Kevin Hilton (born 1962); and Ronald Jeffrey Hilton (born 1963). Paris's father, Rick Hilton (born 1955), was third from the youngest in the pack.

It didn't take Barron long to rise (both figuratively and literally) from elevator operator to CEO of several enterprises. In 1954, he was elected a vice president of Hilton Hotels Corporation and also became president of the Carte Blanche credit card firm and was the owner of a $6 million orange juice company, head of a business leasing jets, and an investor in a Texas oil company. Additionally, he founded the Los Angeles Chargers in 1960 and as president of the Hilton Hotel chain was instrumental in getting Hilton Hotels into the gambling business. In the Forbes 400, which lists the 400 richest Americans, Barron Hilton's worth in 2007 is listed at $2.3 billion.

However, when Connie died in 1979, he left bulk of his estate, which involved the controlling interest in the hotel chain, to the Roman Catholic Church and charities and a relative pittance to his children. Not surprisingly, Barron contested the will, claiming that it had a provision that allowed Barron to purchase the stock for the market value at the time of Connie's death, about $165 million. By the time Barron won the case, in the late 1980s, it was worth upwards of $490 million. Half-sister Francesca also sued but lost her case and received nothing.

History repeated itself in 2007, when, supposedly disgusted by Paris's sex tape, incarceration, and assorted public high jinks, Barron himself announced that he would divert approximately 97 percent of his $2.3 billion fortune to the Conrad N. Hilton Foundation. For more than six decades, the charity had distributed $560 million to aid the blind, mentally ill, and homeless; prevent substance abuse; and increase access to safe water in Africa and Mexico. While the money continues to help the work of Catholic sisters; more than half goes to international projects.

The remaining $69 million will be divvied up between the numerous surviving heirs, including 23 grandchildren, which would leave Paris with a mere $5 million. This raised a firestorm of speculation; biographer Oppenheimer was widely quoted in the press as saying, "Barron Hilton was, and is extremely embarrassed by how the Hilton name has been sullied by Paris."

However, Barron himself countered through the Page Six gossip column, stating through a family rep that Oppenheimer was wrong: "I love her very much and am proud of what she has accomplished."[16]

Regardless, she will hardly be destitute. Her reported income in 2006 and 2007 was about $7 million per year, and given her many enterprises, it will likely only increase. Additionally, her real estate mogul father is worth about $300 million, which divided four ways—between Paris, Nicky, and their two younger siblings—comes out to a cool $75 million apiece.

But regardless of how the Hilton elder feels—his announcement came as no surprise to either Paris or Nicky—it all boils down to the strict work ethic that began with Conrad and his descendents. During the 1986 trial contesting Conrad's will, advisor James Bates testified that Connie didn't want to leave "unearned wealth" to his family but rather have them "get out and . . . earn their own living."[17] As indeed they have, raising eyebrows all along the way.

MOM'S SIDE: KEEPING UP APPEARANCES

If the Hilton family was striving, conniving, and ambitious, at least they have money to show for it. Paris's mother's side was equally if not more ruthless, and all they got was celluloid and tabloid exposure, not to mention a veritable graveyard of broken promises, relationships, and marriages. Her grandmother, the "overbearing, determined, and very outlandish" Big Kathy Richards was, according to Hilton biographer Jerry Oppenheimer, the proverbial bad seed, "a mistress of manipulation who dominated and controlled Little Kathy's and her sisters' every professional and personal decision, from the outfits they wore, to the jobs they took, to the men they dated and married."[18]

However, Paris's maternal great-grandparents, lawyer and politico "Big Ed" Dugan and his homemaker wife Dorothy "Dodo" Dugan, were well-regarded, upstanding Catholics who moved from Omaha, Nebraska, to the exclusive suburb of Manhasset, Long Island, shortly after WWII, when Big Kathy, the third of four children, was about 10. The family also speculated in "flipping" houses, buying and refurbishing fixer-uppers and then selling them for a profit.

Kathy quickly made a name for herself at the newly opened grammar school at St. Mary's Roman Catholic Church. "Always in control, always in everyone's face [she] . . . became the leader of an A-list clique at St. Mary's—a small group of snarky, sanitized grade school 'Heathers,' who did everything from intimidate other children to play cruel jokes on them," writes Oppenheimer. Like some of the Hiltons, including Paris herself, Big Kathy bounced from one institution of learning to the next, attending the Academy of St. Joseph, which her older sister Donna also went to. While there that she discovered what she thought was her calling—singing and acting—"and began thinking of herself as a future star."[19]

Eventually, wild Kathy ended up in the Manhasset public high school, chasing her latest obsession, a young man by the name of Bob Conkey, whom she pursued relentlessly through adulthood—even after they'd both wed other people. But they never married each other. "Kathleen and I would drive all over town desperately looking for him and if we found him, he wouldn't give her the time of day," recalls childhood friend Jane Halleran. She always made a fool out of herself . . . when it came to him." And despite Kathy's many marriages, "she was always unhappy in love."[20]

A high school dropout at 16, Kathy had big dreams of fame and fortune, attending the American Academy of Dramatic Arts in New York in 1957, where a more well-known actor named Robert Redford was also a classmate. She didn't graduate, instead falling for Little Kathy's dad, college student and football player Larry Avanzino, who, according to pal Halleran, was "gorgeous and a total maniac."[21]

In a short time Kathy became pregnant and they hastily married, much to the dismay of both sets of parents. Their daughter and Paris's mother, "little" Kathleen Elizabeth Avanzino, was born seven months after the impromptu wedding, on March 13, 1959. The Avanzinos divorced two years later.

But some stardust emanated from that failed union, in the form of Paris's mother, "little" Kathy, a blonde, cute stunner with a china-doll face. Discovered by renowned freelance photographer Constance Bannister, who would also help promote Little Kathy's not-yet-born sisters Kim and Kyle, Little Kathy started her career in modeling as a "Bannister Baby," appearing in national advertising campaigns and eventually TV shows such as *Family Affair*. Not one to remain single for long, Big Kathy got her claws into the man who would eventually be her children's stepfather Ken Richards, a successful developer and marketer of ladies' apparel who had the minor complication of already being married with three children. Richards fell prey to Big Kathy's machinations after they met at a party at his mansion.

Although the Richards' marriage had its problems, when his wife Evelyn found out about the affair, she went to the Long Island bar/restaurant where Kathy worked as a hat-check girl, ostensibly to confront her. At some point, a restaurant employee claimed that Kathy put knockout drops in Evelyn's drink, and, Evelyn's daughter teenaged Diane recalled, "Kathleen . . . followed my mother, who was staggering, trying to get away out to her car." As Evelyn struggled to open the Lincoln Continental's heavy door, "Kathy purposefully slammed the door on her ankle and crushed it." In separate, later incidents with the Richards family, Big Kathy also reportedly put a screw in Diane's cheeseburger when she thought her stepdaughter was undermining her marriage and fed her elderly, frail mother-in-law dog food, laughing hysterically about it. Nevertheless, Diane fell in love with Paris Hilton's future mother: Little Kathy "was just so sweet [and] precious, I used to take her with me all over the place, even to parties. I was so proud of her."[22]

Repeating her earlier pattern, Kathy became pregnant with Ken's love child, Kim, in 1964, resulting in his quickie Mexican divorce from Evelyn and just as hasty remarriage. Although Richards wanted to adopt the toddler Kathy, Big Kathy refused, not wanting to give up control of her little moneymaker. However Richards raised Kathy as his own child, and she did take on his surname, both personally and professionally.

Following in her big sister's footsteps, Kim her made her debut while still in diapers, crawling around for Firth Carpet and Pampers. Around this time the family moved to LA, building a custom home in Bel Air, where Big Kathy continued to tyrannize her husband, daughters, and stepdaughter. By the time Kyle, the third and last of Big Kathy's children, came along in 1968, the marriage had not surprisingly begun a rapid downward spiral, thanks to Big Kathy's excessive spending, drinking, and cheating.

Kim ended up being the most famous of the Richards girls, at least before her niece Paris came along. Little Kathy could boast guest spots on such shows as *The Rockford Files* and *Happy Days,* and Kyle also began a respectable acting career in 1975 as Alicia Sanderson Edwards on the television series *Little House on the Prairie,* subsequently appearing in several television series and horror films, even recently as Nurse Dori on *ER* and in Paris's own series *The Simple Life* and *My New BFF.* But it was Kim who was the real star. Along with talent and good looks, she had a photographic memory, which made it very easy for her to memorize her lines. From 1970–71, she landed the lead of Prudence Everett in the television series *Nanny and the Professor.* She also appeared in several Disney films, including *Escape to Witch Mountain* (1975), *No Deposit, No Return* (1982), and *Return from Witch Mountain* (1978) and also recently in *Black Snake Moan* (2006) and *Race to Witch Mountain* (2009). She later starred in the short-lived series *Hello, Larry* and as a guest on numerous episodes of popular TV classics including *Diff'rent Strokes, Alice, The Love Boat, Little House on the Prairie, ChiPs, Magnum, P.I.,* and many others. With a huge following of fans who took note of her every outfit and boyfriend in the teen press, Kim was a toned-down version of the "It" girl in the 1970s and early '80s, although nothing like the firestorm of publicity that would follow Paris, of whom she was reportedly jealous.

By many accounts Big Kathy was the stage mother from hell, demanding much from her daughters and favoring whichever one would make her the most money, "All of them—Little Kathy, Kyle, and Kim—were always trying to please Mama," states Sylvia Benedict Richards, who eventually became Ken Richard's third and final wife. Kim in particular was obedient to Big Kathy's dictates; picking up her mother at different bars even before she was old enough to get her license and performing skits and dances for her mother's various men friends.[23]

Big Kathy and Ken Richards' divorce became final in 1979, although they had actually separated several years earlier. And while she didn't always practice what she preached when it came to her own relationships, she did instill her golden rule—marry rich and into a prominent family and have lots of children—into her daughters. However, Kim's two marriages, to supermarket scion George Brinson and a really big fish, multibillionaire oil heir Gregg Davis, after whom the fictional Carringtons were modeled in the '80s TV hit *Dynasty*, both ended in divorce. After a first failed try to a wealthy foreigner, Kyle got it right, laying claim to real estate mogul Mauricio Umansky and one-upping her mother by giving birth to four daughters. And there was, of course, Kathy's biggest success story—her eldest's daughter's 1979 nuptials to Rick Hilton. "My daughters are married to men who have a total net worth of $13 billion," she once bragged to friend Linda McKusker.[24] Except for one notable exception described below and which the family denies, Paris herself has had several engagements and failed relationships, all to men who are either wealthy or famous or both.

But Big Kathy didn't always follow her own advice, especially when it came to Jack Catain, "a hot-tempered mobster who had the connections to put out contracts," according to Hilton biographer Oppenheimer.[25] They supposedly wed and divorced twice—the only official record of the union that can be found lists the date as 1980, a good six months after Little Kathy had safely tied the knot with Rick Hilton. Big Kathy and Catain had actually hooked up earlier, but Big Kathy felt the need to distance herself from him, correctly reasoning that the Hilton family's discovery of her association with such a disreputable character might put a damper on her eldest child's upcoming nuptials. Yet when it came to ethics and matters of the heart, Big Kathy and Catain were two peas in the pod; she was out to get all she could, and he didn't care whether he broke the law earning it. Catain was a womanizer as well. However, when they divorced two years later, he actually took money from her, a first for Big Kathy. Kathy took the financial hit—it was a lot safer than an actual one.

But she had one more marriage left in her. After a stint as a shop owner and after unsuccessfully trolling the tony bars of Beverly Hills for available men, she decided to relocate to Palm Springs in the 1990s. Known as "God's Waiting Room" because of all the elderly folk who resided there, it was a playground for the rich and retired. Showing the resourcefulness that would later appear in her granddaughter Paris as she rebounded from her own setbacks, Big Kathy decided to lose weight, get a facelift, and move to a golf course, hoping to snag a rich duffer.

This time her prey—and fourth husband—ended up being the "Silver Fox," Robert Fenton, a widowed aerospace marketing executive whose wife had recently died of uterine cancer. Although Fenton's first marriage had lasted 35 years and he had a plethora of women chasing him, he was somewhat naïve and moved in with Big Kathy shortly after the failure of a disastrous and rapid second marriage to a lounge singer known locally as the "Black Widow." Impressed by the Hilton fame and wealth, "he would always tell me, she's part of the Hiltons, her daughter is Kathy Hilton, her son-in-law is Rick Hilton, his father was Conrad Hilton's son," recounted Fenton's daughter, Judy Goldstone.[26]

In 1998 and around the time of her last marriage, Big Kathy learned that she too had cancer, so Fenton ended up being a caretaker for the second time. She also periodically hosted an unexpected visitor—her teenaged granddaughter, Paris, then in high school. Paris had been shipped from New York for reasons that remain somewhat murky. Her mother claimed it was to avoid a stalker, while workers at the Waldorf-Astoria, where the family lived at the time, stated that Paris had taken off with a good-looking trucker whom she met at the unloading dock of the hotel. Paris's other antics—for example, "borrowing" a friend's parents' car and driving all over the city—and her provocative behavior with boys and at nightclubs undoubtedly also contributed to the banishment.

Regardless of the reason, Big Kathy adored her granddaughter, encouraging her to take up modeling. "My mom always knew that Paris would be where she is [today]," stated Little Kathy. "I don't know how she knew . . . [although] a psychic told her that Paris would be one of the most photographed famous women in the world."[27] And indeed it was in a Beverly Hills condo owned by Big Kathy that Paris struck an infamous, half-naked pose—accompanied by the universal gesture so favored by irate drivers—that was published in the September 2000 issue of *Vanity Fair*; exposure that, in more ways than one, would help propel her into national fame.

And the admiration was mutual—Paris has attributed much of her success to Big Kathy's tutelage. "I really believe my grandma's up there making all this happen for me," she remarked. "She always called me Grace Kelly or Marilyn Monroe and said, 'You're going to be the biggest star in the whole world.' She was the most important person in my life and . . . she comes to me in my dreams. . . . I know she's still watching."[28]

Big Kathy passed away in 2002, leaving Fenton virtually penniless and alone, because the house they shared—which he had invested his savings in—was in her name and her will stipulated that he was forbidden female company during the 12 months after her death that he was allowed to stay there. Fenton died three years later in a trailer park.

In 2005, when Little Kathy was promoting her own reality TV show on etiquette and classy behavior, *I Want to Be a Hilton*, she told a reporter, "My mother would never have dared make anybody feel uncomfortable."[29] This knack for selective memory would serve both her—and her daughter—very well.

RICK AND KATHY: MERGER AND ACQUISITION

Paris's parents, Rick and Kathy, have experienced considerably less drama than their ancestors. Perhaps that's a good thing, given what has happened with Paris and Nicky (Nicholai Olivia, born October 5, 1983) during their teenaged years. Their two younger sons, Barron Nicholas Hilton II (born November 7, 1989) and Conrad Hughes Hilton III (born March 3, 1994), will soon be coming into their own as well with whatever consequences that may bring.

Born August 17, 1955, Rick Hilton grew up in Sorrento Beach, California, in a mansion overlooking the Pacific that had been the abode of silent film star Norma Shearer. His celebrity neighbors included Peter Lawford, a member of the original "Rat Pack," which included Frank Sinatra, Dean Martin, Sammy Davis Jr., and others. His wife, Patricia Kennedy Lawford, was the sister of President John F. Kennedy. Their firstborn, Christopher Kennedy Lawford, was Rick's childhood pal. In high school, he also ran with scions of the showbiz crowd, including Desi Arnaz Jr. (son of Lucille Ball and Desi Arnaz) and Dean Paul Martin, offspring of Dean Martin . . . and also Kathy Richards, whom he started dating when he was 19 and Kathy was 15.

Despite the family's great wealth, Rick's growing-up years were mostly uneventful; in fact, Rick often worked as a bellboy during spring and summer breaks. "The way my dad was raised, his father taught him the value of a dollar," recalled Rick. "He passed that along to myself and I passed that along" to his children.[30] He attended the University of Denver (DU) where he also played volleyball, graduating in December 1978. Although the college had a reputation for being a rich kid's party school, with students ranging from Eurotrash/trustafarians to children of Saudi oil barons to offspring of owners of major corporations like AT&T, Royal Crown Cola, and (of course) Hilton Hotels, Rick took his studies somewhat seriously, majoring and receiving a BA in hotel and restaurant management as well as taking cooking classes.

He also gave fantastic parties, putting to work the self-promotion machine that his daughter Paris would also utilize to her best advantage. The get-togethers had "great bands and great food—not potato chips like your typical college parties and there were *hundreds* of people there," remembers Melanie Gelb, a former classmate. "It was *the* party to be invited to."[31] Also continuing the Hilton tradition of giving away nothing for free, Rick charged $20 a head. And the bashes were held at—but of course—the Denver Hilton.

Although he inherited the Hilton entrepreneurial talents, Rick was somewhat shy with the fairer sex, sticking with "a girl with blond hair who would hang on him like a Christmas ornament, like she was protecting her turf," continued Gelb, who came to believe that the female in question was the future Kathy Hilton.[32]

Rick was also the subject of a faux kidnapping, a college prank cooked up by staff members of the student newspaper *The Clarion*. "It was a slow news week and we were not going to make news kidnapping somebody named Jones," observed then-editor Rob Levin, who went on to work for the *Atlanta Journal-Constitution*. The plan revolved around snatching Rick from the student union, spiriting him away in a borrowed getaway Jeep, and calling campus security and reporting the crime. However, things went awry because "he pitched up such a fit that we just had to let him go. I'm not sure Ricky was in a position to even know what was going on, what with the various beverages he was drinking."[33] Rick and Kathy became serious shortly after his graduation from DU.

On the other hand, Kathy Richard's tender years were somewhat more challenging. In addition to her mother's marital issues and the turmoil caused by the constant pressure to become a star, by the time she was a teenager, Little Kathy's showbiz career had sputtered and died. Her mother had turned her attentions toward the more successful Kim and even Kyle; Kathy was reportedly jealous of Kim. So she did what many normal sixteen-year-olds would do—slept a lot, blew off her studies, and ran around with boys. She attended California Preparatory School, where classmates included members of the Jackson Five family and Danny Bonaduce of *Partridge Family* fame, whose controversial 2005 reality show *Breaking Bonaduce* aired around the same time as Kathy's. She was never much of student, and "Kathy's whole thing was going out and having fun," stated Pierce Jensen, a friend at the time. "And if we weren't going out to the restaurants in West LA, or cruising the Sunset Strip, we would pretty much just hang out at her home." She also "flirted with every guy who crossed her path,"[34] earning a reputation as a tease.

She "dated around" after graduation, with Rick's friends Desi Arnaz Jr. and Dean Paul Martin and, thanks to her mother's connections, spent time with sons of Middle-Eastern oil barons and professional football players as well as at the Playboy Mansion.

Big Kathy accompanied her daughter and her friends on excursions, leading rise to the rumor that she was running an escort service. But

Paris Hilton, left, and Kathy Hilton arrive at the launch party of Paris Hilton's new MTV series, My New BFF, in Los Angeles on September 30, 2008. (AP Photo/Matt Sayles)

the truth was far simpler: "Big Kathy was just like a mother to everybody and she loved all these girls to death and they just flocked to her," asserted Marlene Catain, Mickey Catain's ex-wife. The two women had become friendly after their respective divorces from the mobster. They "hung out and talked and had sleepovers and got dressed to go out together. It was fun."[35]

When she was eighteen, shortly before she finally snagged Rick Hilton, Little Kathy was offered $25,000 to pose in *Playboy* magazine, which back in the late 1970s was a formidable chunk of change. She was ready to accept because it meant a new car and other goodies. Longtime family friend Kay Rozario dissuaded her, correctly pointing out that being "Miss June" or whatever would follow her around for the rest of her life, especially if she wanted to marry into a prestigious family. Then Little Kathy decided to cut a demo record; like her mother before her—and daughter Paris—she was an enthusiastic and some say talented songbird. Kay's husband Bob, a producer for Tony Orlando, the Osmonds, and others had the connections to make career happen, but it never came to fruition. Because by that time her ship had come in and she'd finally landed Rick Hilton.

Although a marriage between an aspiring starlet and the son of a hotel magnate might seem incongruous, each had something to gain. "My take on Rick was that he was enamored of show business and that's why he liked her—she was an arm-piece who would happily hang out with him and do all the rich guy things that he wanted to do," observed veteran reporter Barbara Sternig, who interviewed Little Kathy for the *National Enquirer* shortly before their nuptials. "I thought they were not the brightest light bulbs in the chandelier, so it was a match made in heaven. I never heard anything about Kathy again until Paris became famous."[36]

The Hiltons were married on November 24, 1979, at the Church of the Good Shepherd in Beverly Hills—also known as "Our Lady of the Cadillacs," a nod to the vehicle of choice among its well-to-do flock. It was here that, thirty years earlier, Paris's great-uncle Nick Hilton and Elizabeth Taylor had their short, ill-fated nuptials—"the wedding of the century." Although hardly on the same scale publicity-wise, the Kathy/Rick union has lasted considerably longer, although not all of the Hilton family was thrilled about the blushing bride or her family.

Conrad's father Barron in particular disliked big Kathy, barring her from his home when he was there and calling her "The Madam"—as in one who runs a house of ill-repute. He and Little Kathy had numerous run-ins, especially when he refused to give Rick preferential treatment—something that none of his children received. When it came to business matters, Barron was an equal-opportunity hardass. The Hilton wives were equally leery of Rick's new spouse, pegging her as a social climber and gold digger, although some came from far-from-wealthy backgrounds themselves. In his new daughter-in-law and her mother, Barron may have recognized a cruder form of the same blonde (or in big Kathy's case, red-headed) ambition and ruthlessness that had made his family so successful and would also make them targets as Paris's star began to rise.

In spite or perhaps because of the family's many acquisitions and numerous detractors, starting with Conrad's purchase of the fleabag Mobley hotel in 1919, "the Hilton[s] . . . seem forever plagued by the crisp tint of new money,"[37] observed the 2000 *Vanity Fair* article that helped launch Paris and her younger sister Nicky into the national spotlight—hardly a sterling recommendation for the upper echelons of society. But like her ancestors before her, Paris was hardly one to let critics stop her.

NOTES

1. Paris Hilton with Merle Ginsberg, *Confessions of an Heiress* (New York: Fireside, 2005), 157–66.

2. Conrad Hilton, *Be My Guest* (Englewood Cliffs, NJ: Prentice Hall, 1957), www.hiltonfranchise.com.

3. "Hotels: The Key Man," *Time Magazine* (Dec. 12, 1949), www.time.com/time/magazine/article/0,9171,854077,00.html.

4. Hilton, *Be My Guest.*

5. "Hotels: The Key Man."

6. Jerry Oppenheimer, *House of Hilton* (New York: Random House, 2006), 152.

7. Hilton and Ginsberg, *Heiress*, 10.

8. Oppenheimer, *House of Hilton*, 154.

9. Ibid., 155.

10. Ibid., 178.

11. Ibid., 232.

12. Ibid., 195.

13. Ibid., 240.

14. Hilton and Ginsberg, *Heiress*, 20.

15. Ibid., 33.

16. "Paris, Nicole Simple as Ever," *New York Post* (Aug. 1, 2007): 12.

17. Oppenheimer, *House of Hilton*, 256.

18. Ibid., 27.

19. Ibid., 60.

20. Ibid., 65.

21. Ibid., 69.

22. Ibid., 80–81.

23. Ibid., 94.

24. Ibid., 28.

25. Ibid., 109.

26. Ibid., 128.

27. *Paris, Not France*, directed by Adria Petty, documentary (New York: MTV, 2008), unpublished transcript.

28. Ibid.

29. "Passport to Paris," *Daily Mail* (London) (Nov. 5, 2005), electronic database access [Proquest].

30. *Paris, Not France*.

31. Oppenheimer, *House of Hilton*, 46.

32. Ibid.

33. Ibid., 47.

34. Ibid., 31, 33.

35. Ibid., 39.

36. Ibid., 51.

37. Nancy Jo Sales, "Hip Hop Debs," *Vanity Fair* (Sept. 2000): 350.

Chapter 2

GROWING UP PARIS

Paris was born 15 months after Rick and Kathy's wedding. By that time, Rick had already set off on his career path of selling commercial real estate and, later, the homes of the rich and famous. At the time of Paris's birth, he was employed by Eastdil Reality, Inc., a New York City investment banking firm. He struck out on his own in 1993, forming Hilton Realty Investment, later renamed Hilton & Hyland. Based in Los Angeles, the company not only brokered numerous hotel deals but also residences of celebrities ranging from Paula Abdul to James Woods, providing Paris and her family with many Hollywood connections. Rick's career in real estate and hotel investment also gave the growing family many opportunities to live in New York, Beverly Hills, and the Hamptons as well as travel abroad.

Paris was on film from the very moment she was born; Rick video-taped her birth—as well as that of her siblings—on a camcorder. A nanny initially coined the "Star" nickname, but the family quickly picked up on the child's physical beauty. One relative described the nine-month-old Paris as a "great big fat pretty baby," while another proclaimed her to be "gorgeous—her face was incredible, like a porcelain doll."[1]

A YOUNG AND RESTLESS FAMILY

Kathy was only 20 when Paris was born; Rick was 24. Kathy herself has often remarked that it was great that she had part of her family when she was so young. "We really grew up together, me and Rick," she said. "Meeting that young, marrying that young and having the little girls so young."[2] Barron and Conrad were born considerably later, although Paris and Nicky are about 2½ years apart.

"We were raised like twins," Paris recalled of her early days with her sister. "We look a lot alike; my mom . . . always dressed us alike . . . [and] we grew up together. . . . We knew we were special and different. We were like a couple of cute blond Eloises running around the Plaza, except it was the Waldorf Towers and it wasn't fiction."[3]

As a young child, Paris often appeared with her mother in New York fashion shows, clad in designer clothes and swimwear and often wearing makeup, much to the dismay of some Hilton elders and the more conventional society matrons. But in most family portraits, Paris seems like any other kid, with missing front teeth, awkward limbs, and a ready smile, especially when surrounded by cousins and siblings. Even as a tot, she appears to be mugging for the camera, instinctively angling her best side and striking the "right" pose.

Others, however, have less rosy memories of the growing family, particularly those who worked in the hotel industry. One insider remarked:

> When they were in New York and Paris was just an infant, Kathy and Rick would get one of the women from housekeeping at the New York Hilton to babysit for them. They would leave Paris on Friday and not come back for her until late Sunday. It was a known fact that Kathy and Rick liked to party, and when Kathy was a young mother, she had no qualms about flaunting the Hilton name and taking advantage of it. She let it be known that Rick was going to be "the next Mr. Hilton" so hotel executives were afraid to argue with her.[4]

The Hiltons often showed up at various hotels with their daughters and pets in tow, even though only trained guide dogs were permitted for the "little people," aka regular paying guests. They never thought twice about ignoring the mess left by their animals, and they never, ever said "thank you," according to many who came in contact with them. "Kathy and Rick and the girls looked down their noses at the help and were very judgmental," recalled former Hilton employee Peggy Cusack Yakovlev, who was also a personal assistant to Rick's Uncle Eric. "Paris and Nicky were running loose in the hotel, were always trouble, and the mother always seemed to be coaching them," adding that the nannies and other help who accompanied them looked as though they were being treated badly.[5] Once employees realized who they were, they went out of their way to avoid them, according to some accounts.

Diane Willgrass, a former nanny to Paris and Nicky, claims to have aged 10 years during a three-week European vacation when the girls were nine and seven, respectively. Willgrass actually worked for the family for about the same amount of time and quit in 2000 with hopes of selling her own "Nanny Diary," a yet to be published tell-all about her experience chez Hilton. Along with the charges of excessive spending—according to her, the girls received $300 a day during

Paris Hilton poses with her father, Rick Hilton, during a press day to promote the second season of the MTV reality show, Paris Hilton's My New BFF *in Los Angeles, May 15, 2009. (AP Photo/ Chris Pizzello)*

the vacation while Kathy's daily allotment was $1,000—and that the "obnoxious children" misbehaved so badly she was forced to spend all her time with them at the park—she leveled the more serious accusation of animal neglect, an allegation that would undoubtedly horrify Paris, an avid creature-itarian. Willgrass maintained that not only did the Hilton pets not get fed, but that she ended up having to bury several. The menagerie of designer dogs and cats as well as hamsters, rabbits, and other assorted critters "stood a better chance of survival" on Sunset Boulevard. Additionally, young Paris made no bones about "let[ing] everybody know who she is. Once I wanted to show her how to make her own bed. She said, 'I'm Paris Hilton. I'll have maids to do that.'"[6]

When someone becomes famous, critics come out of the woodwork. This was true when the upstart Texan Conrad purchased the Waldorf-Astoria in the 1940s, and it happened again, over 50 years later, when his great-granddaughters Paris and Nicky burst onto the scene. Taki Theodoracopulos, playboy and ultraconservative chronicler of the rich and famous whose column "High Life" has appeared in the London *Spectator* since the late 1970s, likened Rick and Kathy Hilton as "straight out of *The Beverly Hillbillies*. They eat hamburgers covered with ketchup washed down with Chateau Latour, live in a large flat in the Waldorf-Astoria which is decorated in early-Eisenhower style, and entertain extremely democratically. By this I mean they have their servants sit down with their guests during meals ('Yo, Rick, pass down the mustard'),"[7] in essence contradicting others' declarations of the Hilton as snobs.

Rick and Kathy "are not about to win the Parenting of the Year award," he continued. Paris and Nicky "wore haute-couture outfits when kids their age were still donning baseball caps and volleyball uniforms. They became famous for preening almost nude for the cameras at every opportunity, including funerals."[8]

Those closer to the family have kinder memories. "Paris had every animal you could think of as a child," stated one relative. "She had so many ferrets, dogs, cats, it would be nothing for her to stick a mouse in your purse and wait for a reaction."[9] Holidays were a big thing among the Hiltons, especially when they were in LA, where many of the cousins resided. Christmas meant ornate decorations in each room of whatever home they were living in, and each Easter the family hosted a big egg hunt, including candy, chocolate, and live animals that were later adopted as pets.

Paris herself gives voice to vivid childhood recollections, which are also at odds with what has appeared in the press:

> When I was growing up, my parents were very strict, especially my mother. We were brought up to be very humble. The rumor is that I got a credit card at age nine, which is ridiculous. It was more like nineteen, and I had to get one myself without my parents. We had rules and regulations. Even when Nicky and I started going out as teenagers in New York, our parents kept a close eye on us. We had to check in with them like ten times a day. I had a curfew of midnight until I was seventeen. People think my parents let us do whatever we wanted but that wasn't true at all. . . . I got punished as much as anyone.[10]

According to her mother Kathy, Paris was entrepreneurial from childhood. "We would make . . . cookies and she would go outside and sell them!" Never one to limit her horizons, especially when it came to branding, little Paris also peddled juice, gum, hair combs, and other things to family and friends.[11]

When the girls were ages eight and five, Paris also managed to con Nicky out of her birthday money. "Nicky's godfather . . . was my dad's best friend," Paris remembered. "He would always give her a hundred dollars on my birthday (Where was *my* hundred dollars?). I soon realized that if I got a toy that Nicky wanted, I could sell it to her" for that Ben Franklin.[12] Thus enterprising Paris was able to get rid of a surplus plaything, purchase something she desired, and still turn a profit.

Paris speaks fondly of her parents, deeming it "cool" (as opposed to her trademark "That's hot!") that they married and had kids at such a young age and that the union has endured. "So many of my friends were only children, and many of them had divorced parents—so I definitely knew how lucky I was to have a sister and both parents around all the time," she said. "My dad supports me in everything I do. My mom's the best, and she's been there for me through everything."[13]

Despite allegations to the contrary, Paris's earliest memories of animals revolve around caring for them. "My dad is an animal lover, like me. He took me to exotic pet shows when I was a kid, and he bought me whatever animal I wanted. . . . My parents still have a ton of dogs and cats at their house in the Hamptons." Paris even kept the baby chicks that she got during Easter "until they turned into roosters—then they'd grow these gross red things on their heads and under their beaks and they'd cock-a-doodle-do every morning at dawn. Our neighbors in Bel Air didn't appreciate that. So I had to give them away."[14] One of her favorite childhood pets was a ferret named Farrah (named after a cousin, not the late Farrah Fawcett).

Initially Paris wanted to be a veterinarian, until "I realized you had to give them shots and put them to sleep so I decided to just buy a bunch of animals and have them at my house instead," she said. She also collected snakes and frogs, "I was a tomboy. I loved digging tunnels in the backyard."[15] Paris also took up ice skating, and like her dad, played some ice hockey while in school.

SCHOOL DAZE

Even before she attended first grade, Paris had an interest in singing; and when she was 10 years old, she appeared in *Wishman* (1992), a forgettable fantasy romance about a genie in search of his bottle. She and Nicky are not even credited, since they were extras—girls on the beach.

By the time the girls were of school age, the family had relocated semi-permanently to Bel Air in Los Angeles. It was here that little brother Barron was born in 1989, while the youngest sibling Conrad would follow five years later, around the time when the Hiltons was moving back to New York City and just as Paris was entering her early teens.

Academics never were a big thing with the Hilton family, although a Catholic education was always deemed important. So Paris and Nicky ended up at the strictly parochial St. Paul the Apostle, which went up to eighth grade. Everyone was required to wear uniforms, and no mixing with boys was allowed. Paris has frequently remarked that her fondness for sexy clothes had as its genesis a rebellion against the conservative, monotonous Catholic school attire. She graduated in June 1995.

Even when they were in their early teen years, before they moved to New York, Nicky and especially Paris stirred up controversy and, in some cases, envy and resentment. "It was hard [for Nicky] to be accepted by the kids—kids that age can be tough," stated Gini Tangalakis, whose daughter Diana was a frequent guest at the Hilton home. "Nicky wasn't included in a lot because she was rich, because she had the Hilton name . . . so all of that made it difficult."[16]

According to some LA friends, Paris started going out when she was 13, and rumors of her sneaking into clubs, claiming that she was 22, and running around with boys swirled around her. "Paris already had a reputation" at St. Paul, continued Tangalakis. "She was off-the-wall even back then."[17] Paris started high school at Marymount in Bel Air, but that was cut short when the family moved to New York City in 1996, into a huge suite at the Waldorf at considerably below the market price, thanks to Rick's connection with the Hilton-owned property.

Paris's recollections, however, are far more innocent.

> When we were on the verge of becoming teenagers, Nicky and I started getting into trouble. Not big-time trouble, just your normal kid stuff. . . . We'd make prank phone calls, leave messages for dogs on answering machines, and silly stuff like that. . . . When we were a little older and lived in the Waldorf, we once dressed up and snuck into a ball—no one knew it was us. We'd dance around and act all cute, and it didn't occur to anyone to throw us out. I think the hotel staff was afraid of us, even though we were just children.[18]

The move was not as easy or exciting as it appeared, at least at first. "New York and LA are very different," Paris said. "I cried. I thought I was gonna hate it here."[19]

Taking a cue from her family, Paris could also be demanding of the hotel help: "She'll, like roll up to the Waldorf like snap, snap to the desk clerk: 'You give me a key . . .' with a glare in her eye," recalled a friend. "Grabs the key out of their hand, like: 'Tell them to send up room service right now!'"[20]

After a short stint with Nicky at the private, all-female Roman Catholic Convent of the Sacred Heart school, Paris persuaded her parents to enroll her in the more liberal Professional Children's School (PCS), which boasted such attendees as *Home Alone* star Macaulay Culkin and actresses Christina Ricci and Scarlett Johansson. However, the sisters' influence at Sacred Heart was not lost on a younger class-mate, Stefani Joanne Germanotta, who later rose to international fame as the avante-garde pop princess Lady GaGa. "Paris and Nicky Hilton [were] very pretty, and very, very clean," stated Stefani/GaGa. "It's im-pressive to be that perfect all the time. In commercial terms, they've been quite an influence on me."[21]

And the admiration turned out to be mutual, although Paris was five years ahead of GaGa and probably never even crossed paths with her in Sacred Heart's hallowed halls. "Her outfits are so amazing!" Paris tweeted. "She is such a style icon! No one can pull it off like she can!" In 2009, she spoke with Gaga backstage in London, posing and posting multiple pictures of her with the singer and praising her musical ability. "Lady Gaga looks so hot! Love her!"[22]

Even the thought of Paris in anything resembling a convent seems like an oxymoron. And given her hopes of becoming a model and singer, PCS's focus on careers in arts, entertainment, and competitive athletics seemed like a better fit than the rigorous intellectual curricu-lum and rigid adherence of Sacred Heart. However, even PCS became a bit too serious and competitive as Paris (and Nicky) were starting to become regulars on the New York club circuit, which didn't jibe well with the demands and discipline required of a serious artist. So by the time she was a junior, Paris transferred to the exclusive and expensive Dwight School, a private institution in Central Park West.

Founded in 1872 and once the institution of choice for scions of the elite New York upper crust, Dwight had fallen somewhat far down the social pantheon by the mid-1990s, when Paris was a student there. It had developed a reputation for being a dumping ground for spoiled rich kids, not unlike Rick's alma mater, the University of Denver. In fact Dwight was locally known as "Dumb White Idiots Getting High Together," and apparently Paris didn't fit in there, either.

"Paris was sort of more sophisticated," observed a classmate. "She was different from everybody else. But she was always, like, really nice. . . . She looked like a Barbie doll and other kids didn't know how to react to it."[23] Paris attended Dwight until her senior year, when she was whisked off to California to live with her grandmother, either due to her antics or to escape a stalker, depending upon which version the reader wants to believe.

After she was pulled from Dwight, Kathy also claimed that Paris went to with live with the family for a time at the London Hilton, where she was privately tutored. However, while with her grandmother, she enrolled at the ritzy Palm Valley School in Rancho Mirage, where she showed up in algebra class with a bejeweled calculator. She matriculated at other institutions at various points throughout her high school career: the Canterbury School in Connecticut, where she was promptly kicked out after going AWOL for a weekend, and the Buckley School in Sherman Oaks, California. "At Buckley, all the guys loved her," Kimberly Stewart, daughter of singer Rod Stewart and a friend of Paris, recalled. "Because, you know, we had to wear uniforms . . . and there's a certain way you had to wear your skirt . . . and I'd kind of lift mine up and she'd lift hers up a little further and our skirts would be a little shorter than everyone else's and we always used to get in trouble for that."[24]

During her time at Canterbury, Paris had a brief if wobbly career on the hockey team. Rather than knocking people over, she was more concerned about falling down and complained the safety helmet hurt her head. When former teammate and Canterbury hockey captain Stacy Burns White helped Paris remove the helmet, "I saw she had a banana clip [keeping her hair in place]," said White. "They're rather big underneath the helmet. I told her, 'We need to take the banana clip out.' Paris responded, 'What am I supposed to do about my hair?' She clearly didn't understand how this all worked."[25]

Paris has attributed her lack of scholastic enthusiasm to attention deficiency disorder, which she claimed she'd been diagnosed with as a child. According to some sources, she allegedly obtained a GED from the Dwight School and decided to further her education informally, in the college of hard knocks. Which might not have been a bad idea, especially since both she and Nicky seemed to suffer at the expense of what her aunt Kyle Richards believed to be jealous classmates. "They're beautiful, they're rich, they have the last name Hilton," observed Richards. And once people found that out, it didn't help with "making a lot of friends with girls. [Paris] always had this attitude that she didn't care what people thought but she definitely did."[26]

SISTER ACT, PART 1

Nowhere are Paris's feelings closer to the surface than when discussing her sister Nicky. She describes her as her best friend, her unofficial twin, and an unswerving source of support. The sisters have been each other's constant companions, even living together in their late teens/early twenties when Nicky decided to move from New York to Hollywood. They look alike—tall, thin, with radiant smiles and flawless skin, sparkling blue eyes, and gleaming teeth—have many of the same mannerisms, and even dress alike; Kathy bought two of nearly every outfit when they were growing up, a practice the girls continued through their young adulthood.

The resemblance was especially striking when Nicky was a blonde, although in recent years she's been brunette or variations thereof, perhaps to differentiate herself from Paris, who has embraced the limelight while Nicky has backed away from it somewhat. The two sisters remain inseparable even today, traveling the world together and gadding about Hollywood.

Paris Hilton, left, and sister Nicky Hilton arrive at the MTV Movie Awards in Universal City, CA, on June 6, 2010. (AP Photo/Chris Pizzello)

As a tot, Paris recalled being thrilled when she found out that her mom was pregnant with Nicky and, after the baby was born, claimed never to have been jealous, appreciating the fact that she now had a companion, rather than being an "only lonely" child like so many of her friends. Like any sisters, they argued, but they also figured out early on that they needed to present a united front. When they were little, Paris remembered Nicky busting her to their mom for swearing. Paris pulled Nicky aside and explained "that it was us against them, that we two girls were a team. . . . We had to stay loyal to each other."[27]

They enjoyed the usual childhood antics: rollerblading around the driveway, jumping on beds, playing dress-up. They even created a little boutique in their bedroom and, capitalizing on the Hilton sense of enterprise, attempted to convince family and friends to shell out cash for their stuff, making it Paris's first memorable experience with stores and shopping, although it would hardly be her last. They also played "pretend"—with Nicky as the princess and Paris the queen, as she was the older (and bossier) of the two. At just 12 years old, Nicky got her first job working as an intern with *Hamptons Magazine*, which mostly consisted of the pre-teen running errands and taking lunch orders.

They helped each other in school as well. Paris loved art class, while Nicky preferred writing, creating a mutual aid society when it came to homework. But perhaps best of all, and guaranteeing sisterly love, was the fact that they had and continue to have opposite tastes in men. Unlike some sisters, "we never, ever liked the same guy," said Paris. Nicky "is the one girl I've always trusted with my boyfriends, no matter what. Our bond is stronger than any bond either of us could have with a guy."[28]

Paris also relied on Nicky when it came to another matter to of earth-shattering importance to her—fashion. The younger Hilton sister's taste was so notable that, at age 15, she was voted as one of the best-dressed women in the world by *Vogue* magazine. "She's better at shopping than I am. . . . I get bored fast, and I wear more costumey clothes—wild, crazy, funky stuff from all kinds of shops," remarked Paris. "Nicky's more sophisticated—she only wears high-fashion designers, and she prefers bigger, fancier stores." And perhaps even best of all and very important to image-conscious Paris: "She always tells me the truth about which outfit looks best."[29] Paris has eliminated *Best Friend Forever* (BFF) TV show contenders based on their lack of fashion sense and candor regarding her wardrobe.

Not surprisingly, the tall, blonde Hilton sisters were a huge and immediate sensation in Japan, one of their favorite places to go shopping. As teenagers, they spent major retail time in the mega-malls in Tokyo and still visit there regularly to promote their various brands, from handbags to perfumes to shoes. "The Japanese love us," Paris went on. "Nicky and I have to wear black wigs and we can't even walk next to each other." When they want to hit the stores, they even split up so as not to recognized and mobbed by screaming fans, most of whom are female. But even in disguise, if they are together, groupies somehow figure out that the Hilton sisters are in the house and rush forward for an autograph, behavior Paris finds ironic, considering that country's emphasis on reserved and polite behavior.[30]

Yet throughout the years, each sister has retained her own distinct personality. "Nicky is . . . quieter than I am and probably more serious," observed Paris. Nicky is also "a little more strict and uptight with her friends than I am, and she's definitely shyer."[31]

But that works well because Nicky, whom Paris also claims has a wicked sense of humor, serves as a touchstone and reality check. As Nicky herself observed, when Paris steps too deeply into her blonde "heirhead" role, "Sometimes I tell her, like, stop. Someone will ask her a question and she'll say, 'I don't know.' But I know she knows."[32]

Although the sisters profess undying loyalty and admiration for each other, they undoubtedly recognize that had there not been two of them, and had they not been so wealthy, blonde, and good-looking, they might have never have been noticed. When the teenagers burst upon the New York club scene, the "hip hop debs" as they were dubbed, were the talk of the town and the center of a whirlwind of gossip and speculation. It was like having two beauties for the price of one. The addition of Nicole Richie, a childhood friend and the daughter of singer Lionel Richie, stirred up even more controversy and set a chain of events into motion, news which would reach even the most distant outposts of America.

NOTES

1. Chas Newkey-Burden, *Paris Hilton: Life on the Edge* (London: John Blake, 2007), 10.

2. Ibid.

3. Paris Hilton with Merle Ginsberg, *Confessions of an Heiress* (New York: Fireside, 2005), 20.

4. Jerry Oppenheimer, *House of Hilton* (New York: Random House, 2006), 15.

5. Ibid., 16.

6. Ann O'Neill, "City of Angles," *LA Times* (March 12, 2001): E2.

7. Taki, "Talk of the Town," *The Spectator* (London) 293, 9146 (Nov 22, 2003): 76.

8. Ibid.

9. Newkey-Burden, *Paris Hilton*, 17.

10. Hilton and Ginsberg, *Heiress*, 157.

11. Newkey-Burden, *Paris Hilton*, 16.

12. Hilton and Ginsberg, *Heiress*, 29.

13. Ibid., 158.

14. Ibid., 166.

15. Newkey-Burden, *Paris Hilton*, 16.

16. Oppenheimer, *House of Hilton*, 18–19.

17. Ibid.

18. Hilton and Ginsberg, *Heiress*, 30.

19. Nancy Jo Sales, "Hip Hop Debs," *Vanity Fair* (Sept. 2000): 379.

20. Ibid., 356.

21. Carlos Baez, "Lady GaGa Influenced by Ex-Convent Paris Hilton," igossip.com (January 17, 2009), igossip.com/gossip/Lady_GaGa_Influenced_By_Ex_Convent_Paris_Hilton_Nicky_ Hilton/532157.

22. "Yawn: Paris Hilton Calls Lady Gaga a 'Fashion Icon,'" Reel Loop (December 27, 2009), blog.reelloop.com/5295/celeb/yawn-paris-hilton-calls-lady-gaga-fashion-icon/.

23. Ibid., 379.

24. Oppenheimer, *House of Hilton*, 24.

25. Joe Kovacs, "Paris Hilton Was High-School Hockey 'Sensation,'" *PhotoNetDaily* (June 14, 2007), www.wnd.com/?pageId=42071.

26. Newkey-Burden, *Paris Hilton*, 25.

27. Hilton and Ginsberg, *Heiress*, 20, 24.

28. Ibid., 29.

29. Ibid., 31.

30. *Paris, Not France*, directed by Adria Petty, documentary (New York: MTV, 2008), unpublished transcript.

31. Hilton and Ginsberg, *Heiress*, 24, 31.

32. *Paris, Not France*.

Chapter 3

NICKY AND NICOLE

The third piece of what helped create the Paris Hilton persona involves yet another young woman, Nicole Richie, the adopted daughter of singer Lionel Richie and his ex-wife Brenda. While some accounts place the fateful meeting of Paris and Nicole when Nicole was in kindergarten at the Buckley School in Sherman Oaks, California, others claim they met while still toddlers. Regardless, the friendship sparked a combustion of creativity early on. During their childhood, Paris recalled:

> Lionel had a jukebox and we would lip-synch the songs it played. Nicky, Nicole and I would put on makeup and dance to Tina Turner, Whitney Houston, Madonna, and Prince. We would get all decked out in my mom's clothes and jewelry; then we'd do the show at parties for our parents. It was pretty cute![1]

But Paris and Nicole were also double trouble. "When we were little, our parents always wanted to separate us," Nicole observed. "And I remember . . . them saying, it's not that it's me and not that it's her. It was the two of us together."[2]

Added Paris:

We were like sisters from the moment we met. Once when we
were 12 or 13 and we were in Vegas, we went on the Strip with
our friends from high school. We were walking around and we
couldn't get a cab, so we saw some cops and asked, "Hi, can we
have a ride home?" They said, "How old are you?" and we said,
"Eighteen." My parents got a call saying, "Paris and Nicole are out
on the streets."[3]

Later down the road, however, Paris and Nicole would part ways,
not even speaking to each other for a while, becoming "frenemies,"
that uniquely 21st-century combination of rivalry and closeness. Or,
as Paris has often been quoted as saying, "Keep your friends close, but
your enemies closer."

SISTER ACT, PART DEUX

Paris, Nicky, and Nicole would hit the streets again many times, with
and without the help of the gendarmes. Only now the world would be
watching—and not just their folks. But before Paris and Nicole were
to become a media sensation, Paris and Nicky needed to make their
mark.

When the girls moved back to New York, Paris was almost 16 and
Nicky was two years younger. Like her big sis, Nicky looked much
older than her age and appeared fashion-forward and sophisticated,
although Paris gravitated more toward trendy, flashy, and sexy attire.
And like Paris, Nicky was initially less than thrilled with the move—at
first. "Everything was . . . different," Nicky remarked. "Like when I was
in LA in seventh grade we would just all sit home on a Friday night
and watch movies and . . . make up dances, and in New York there's
house parties and boys."[4] But they hardly stayed put: friends claimed
that Paris started going out as a pre-teen, claiming she was 22 and getting away with it. And there was that escapade in Vegas with Nicole
Richie.

But while Paris and her sister may have just been another two "kids
of" entertainment moguls, film stars, or wealthy heirs in the LA high

school scene, New York touched a match to the fuel of Paris's ambition. "I loved Marilyn Monroe and Madonna," stated Paris. "They were strong influences on me. They knew how to become icons. I realized that's what I wanted to be."[5]

So the two girls started going out nearly every night, occasionally with but mostly without their parents. The latter involved a bit of subterfuge: Ever the planner, Paris scoped out the locations of video cameras at the Waldorf so she and Nicky could slip out undetected. To further assure their anonymity, they donned brown wigs so as not to be recognized by hotel staff. They also pulled the time-honored stunt of putting pillows on their beds so it would look like they were asleep should their parents check on them.

Along with attending exclusive parties and social events, Paris and Nicky popped up frequently at nightclubs—new, old, and just emerging social hot spots like Moomba, Lotus, Spa, and Eugene's, stepping out of a limo all glitzed up and glamorous, blazing past the lines of eager wannabes and trendies waiting anxiously outside the door just hoping to get in. Except for one or two notable occasions—when Paris and/or Nicky became upset because they or their friends were denied access, which always seemed to make the Page Six gossip column in the *New York Post* or the tabloids anyway—the girls were invariably allowed entry to the dance floor and VIP area by the intimidating bouncer. (The bigger the guy, the harder they fall, especially when hot chicks are involved.) They made frenemies with the girls and made out with grunge singers and the boyfriends of others.

Writer Peter Sheridan, veteran chronicler of the celebrity scene, observed of the teenaged Paris and Nicky, with their microminis, four-inch Manolo Blahnik heels and bright lip gloss, "Though both Lolitas are under the legal drinking age, the duo launched themselves on America's nightlife with a vengeance, strutting their way past every velvet rope and into every star-studded VIP room with an open bar."[6]

They started feuds, such as with Stella and Lola Schnabel, daughters of famous painter Julian Schnabel, who were their same ages. The young women competed over who got their picture in the *New York Post* at the earliest age and sniped at each others' outfits, at who looked older and most sophisticated, and who got into the most exclusive club before the other. "[Paris] and Nicky are like partners in bitch crime,"

Hosts Paris Hilton and Nicole Richie open the 2004 Teen Choice Awards in Universal City, CA, on August 8, 2004. (AP Photo/Matt Sayles)

remarked another friend. "It's like the battle of the society sisters."[7] All seems foolishness, but it got them attention. They also made the scene (or in some cases, made a scene with) other rich and/or famous offspring: Casey Johnson of Johnson & Johnson fame, who died tragically in 2010; Amanda Hearst of the media mogul dynasty; debutante Marissa Bregman; Kimberly Stewart, daughter of Rod; LuLu Johnson, daughter of Betsy; and of course, Nicole Richie. She made good friends with "rocker chics" and supermodels—Fergie, Carmen Electra, and especially Naomi Campbell, in 2001 flying to St. Tropez to attend Naomi's 31st birthday party.

Paris and Nicky's antics snagged the interest and speculation of not only fellow partygoers, socialites, and celebrities but also the media; specifically, Richard Johnson, gossip columnist for the *New York Post's* Page Six. These included but were hardly limited to dancing on tables and singing in skimpy clothing (Paris, on several occasions), drinking champagne out of a bottle with a straw (an underage Nicky), and chasing a limo full of Playboy models so she could join in whatever party they were headed to (Paris). Following in the footsteps of her maternal grandmother, Big Kathy; her mother; and skirt-chasing great-uncle

Nick Hilton, Paris would later become a fixture at the Playboy Mansion in LA, singing "Happy Birthday" a la Marilyn Monroe to Hugh Hefner's JFK on the occasion of Hef's 80th in 2006. For a time, she also shared an LA apartment with Playmates Nicole Lenz (March 2000) and Jennifer Rovery (July 1999).

Page Six's Johnson holds the perhaps dubious honor of having written more stories—both positive and negative—about the emerging celebrity of the Hilton sisters than anyone else, tagging Paris as the first "celebutante." "When we first started writing about her, people would question why we were covering a girl who does little else than go to parties and get her picture taken," remarked Johnson. "Now that she's become this international celebrity who is making millions of dollars, I feel that our judgment has been vindicated."[8]

For Paris and Nicky, especially in the beginning, it was all about seeing and being seen. "They're little stars," remarked Jason Binn, publisher of *Hamptons Magazine*, of the girls when they were teenagers hitting the New York club scene. "To them, it's like a job. I believe they wake up every morning and say, 'OK, where am I supposed to be tonight?'"[9]

Paris has readily admitted to teaching herself how to pose for the camera to get the best angle possible. She perfected her trademark catwalk saunter through her experience as a model, signing with the T Management agency, owned by another well-known entrepreneur, family friend Donald Trump, who remarked, "Paris is someone who really understood from an early age the meaning of the word 'celebrity.' She understood what it meant and that it had great value."[10]

She honed her strut under the tutelage of the late Willi Ninja, a renowned performance artist and the inspiration for Madonna's 1990 hit song and music video, "Vogue," who also coached androgynous singer Grace Jones as well as supermodels Naomi Campbell and Christy Turlington. Of teaching the teenaged Paris, Ninja, whose real name was William Leake, observed, "She's a sweet girl [but] I think her attitude is, 'I'm Paris Hilton, everyone's paying for my looks and my name, I really don't care.' How do you get through to somebody that has everything?"[11] Coincidentally, Ninja was also a prominent figure in the documentary *Paris Is Burning*—the city, not the Hilton heir—a film about the transgender and minority ball culture of New York City in the 1980s.

Apparently Paris was a quicker study than she initially seemed, because along with being part of New York Fashion Week, she appeared in fashion shows for designers Marc Bouwer and Catherine Malandrino and ads for Iceberg Jeans. And as they grew older and more polished, both she and Nicky were invited to walk runways in New York and LA, for designers like Joey & T and Jeremy Scott. And of course, this experience would serve as building block for the girls' budding ambitions to design their own line of purses, shoes, and other attire.

Paris was reportedly thrilled when, at age 16, she saw the first photograph of herself and Nicky in the newspapers in the "Best Dressed" fashion section of the *New York Post*. Nevertheless, of those early days, she insisted, "It wasn't that crazy. Any kid who was, like, 16 and allowed into clubs and was invited would go. But . . . the media would tell the story 10 times worse. All I was doing was dancing in a club! Who cares?"[12]

Obviously a growing number of people, especially young males, cared. Paris had several relationships and flirtations with band boys and budding movie and TV stars, no few of which would become the stuff of legend, Internet and otherwise. One sleazy standout, Rick Salomon, dated a teenaged Paris while in his mid-thirties, allegedly meeting her in 2000. The ex-husband of actresses Elizabeth Daily, Shannen Doherty, and Pamela Anderson, he also had numerous liaisons and involvements with assorted actresses, models and Playmates. But as Paris was to find out the hard way, celebrity attracts opportunists like a moth to a flame. "All of a sudden, everyone started paying attention and talking," observed Paris. "I was just going out. I think it's like a dream fantasy people have of heiress sisters."[13] People like to believe that the lives of the rich and famous are more glamorous than their own, and in the case of Paris and Nicky it was (and remains) undoubtedly true.

Paris went on to correctly point out that a few well-placed mentions went a long way toward piquing public interest, particularly as she and Nicky came of legal age and could travel to hot spots in Vegas and LA and at film festivals and anywhere else the young, rich, and beautiful congregated. Along with Page Six, these incidents received coverage in *US Weekly* and the gossip columns of newspapers and magazines—first in the United States and then in the UK, Japan, and elsewhere.

THE FAMILY THAT GETS FAMOUS TOGETHER . . . ALSO GETS CRITICIZED

Around the turn of this century, when Nicky and especially Paris were achieving recognition as "It" girls, the Internet had come into its own as a font of information—useless and otherwise, celebrity and more. Hollywood gossip Web sites such as E!Online, Gawker, PopBitch, and TMZ were burgeoning, providing a fertile proving ground for those brave enough to subject themselves to whatever speculation and possibly even slander the Internet would eventually reap. In 2004, one admirer and friend, born Mario Armando Lavandeira, would reinvent himself in the highest form of flattery, as Perez Hilton, starting a wildly popular and controversial blog known as PageSixSixSix.com, later renamed Perezhilton.com.

Paris and Nicky's visibility was further raised by appearances and profiles on MTV's *Spring Break*, *Celebrity Uncensored*, and part of the *It's Good To Be* . . . independently produced TV series. Capitalizing on her upbringing, Paris made her first credited movie debut in 2000, in *Sweetie Pie*, another independently produced thriller about overprivileged teenagers in LA, written and directed by Asher Levin. In 2001, she appeared as herself in the movie *Zoolander*. As any professional artist knows, drawing from personal experiences or at least a reasonable facsimile is usually a safe bet when starting out in the entertainment business. The E! Entertainment network proved to be a font of all things sisters Hilton, where they would later be the subject of on *E! True Hollywood Story* (THS) on trust-fund babies (2004) and a year later on themselves exclusively.

But the initial piece de resistance that helped emblazon the sisters and especially Paris both in the public mind and among the cognoscenti was a photo essay in the September 2000 issue of *Vanity Fair*, a magazine that specializes in controversial celebrity exposés, in both the literal and figurative senses of the word. Paris was no exception: in this issue, the 19-year-old stood next to her sister and a Rolls Royce a la Lady Godiva, blonde extensions hanging down over her bare chest and a gold necklace stating "rich." Along with an intimate written profile of life chez Hilton, including interviews with Kathy, Rick, and the two younger brothers at their home in the Hamptons, another photo featured a half-naked Paris (the legal half) at Big Kathy's house in Beverly Hills, giving the camera a rude gesture more common to irritated drivers. Along with discussing Paris's romantic link with major heartthrob and then-edgy bad boy Leonardo DiCaprio, extra sizzle was added by pointing out that Paris named her pet Pomeranian Sebastian after the character in the movie *Cruel Intentions* who took advantage of a girl so he could sleep with his own stepsister.

This was, of course, was BT—Before Tinkerbell, her beloved two-pound teacup Chihuahua "accessory dog" who would become almost as famous as her owner. Tinkerbell would eventually "author" her own book and would be the subject of a 2004 "kidnapping" and reappearance, which was never fully explained.

But when the *Vanity Fair* profile was published, all eyes were on Paris and, to some extent, the more toned-down Nicky, who, one wag sniped, at least wasn't hanging from the chandeliers like her big sis. "There's something magnetic about [Paris]," observed Michelle Lee, author of the book *Fashion Victim*. "Part of the reason is the aura of scandal around her. . . . She's sort of a bad girl [with] this faux sexy look on her face."[14]

Once people began to recognize her, Paris discovered that even taking the subway could cause a major stir. She rarely took public transportation, and usually only in winter, when she claimed it smelled less like pee than in the warm months when the rats also came out to play (she found ferrets cute but rats, not so much). Nevertheless she acknowledged the subway as the fastest way to get around New York City, and while people might have expected her to see her emerging from a limo or even perhaps slumming it by taking a taxi, she enjoyed their startled reactions whenever they encountered her on the train.

Every detail about her became the subject of public scrutiny, from her famous blonde tresses—which, incredibly, are naturally curly and of varying lengths, depending on whether hair extensions are involved—to her size 11 feet. "I can't believe people care about what shoe size I wear!" she exclaimed. "I'm not a guy," although it definitely does limit her selection to high heels and certain kinds of boots; she claims that flats, ballet slippers, and tennis shoes make her feet look like canoes.[15]

Yet it was inevitable that all the fame and attention would have a dark side. Rather than being allowed to make the mistakes of normal teenagers—whether it be choosing the wrong boyfriend, experimenting with alcohol and drugs, or even wearing skimpy clothes—every misstep and faux pas was eagerly reported: Paris going ballistic over a boyfriend who spent a little too much time with strippers at a club. Paris berating a security guard who asked for her identification, saying everyone should know who she was: "I don't need ID!" she reportedly screamed at the guard. "Don't you guys ever read the newspaper? Can you even read?"[16] Nicky disrupting a performance by a rock band at an exclusive party at the Sundance Film Festival; Paris supposedly stealing makeup at the same festival. Both girls drinking too much, Paris exposing too much, and Nicky smoking. The reports of their antics went on and on.

Such actions are considered unseemly for normal teenagers, not to mention debutantes who are supposed to be pillars of society and its future leaders (or at least their spouses). There was no need for a coming-out party for these two, since they were already out every night. Family members and social critics weighed in, criticizing Rick and Kathy for allowing and even encouraging lenient behavior and describing the girls as out-of-control teenagers.

"It's all pure porn, and tasteless," sniffed the girls' great-aunt, Francesca Hilton, of the *Vanity Fair* piece. "I was so shocked, it left me speechless. I mean, what was Paris's mother thinking . . . allowing her to do this?" And of Nicky: "What is [Kathy] doing, letting a 16-year-old go nightclubbing on a schoolday? Lesser kids are asked for their IDs and get busted for underage drinking."[17]

However, Francesca, the offspring of patriarch Conrad and actress Zsa Zsa Gabor, was no stranger to bizarre behavior herself. In her younger days, she reportedly went skinny dipping in the pool of the Washington Hilton—the one down the street from the White House—and also spent time in a mental institution, after being disowned by her father and suing his estate over her (relatively) meager $100,000 inheritance. In 2005, Francesca was the subject of a lawsuit from Gabor and her husband Frederick Von Anhalt, claiming that she had forged her mother's signature to take out a $2 million loan by using Gabor's $14 million home as collateral.

"I'm ashamed that Paris and Nicky are related to me," added Celestine Hines, a fourth-generation Hilton.[18] Other family members went even further, accusing Kathy of encouraging the girls to do anything they could to get attention, including tarting up Paris as a toddler by putting makeup on her. One even exclaimed that the Hilton name has been tarnished forever; "[Paris] makes her great-uncle Nick seem like a saint."[19]

But Paris and Nicky quickly rose to their parents' defense. Both girls have insisted that Kathy and Rick were strict with them, limiting their money and making them check in frequently, not to mention earning their own way so they could support themselves, even paying their own parking tickets (rather than sending them to Mom and Dad for "fixing"). And perhaps the most telling incident about the strong family ties occurred when a teenaged Paris came home late one night after sneaking out and found a very worried Kathy sitting on her bed, crying. Paris recalls being devastated over seeing her mom so hurt and upset: "I'm like, 'Oh, no, I'm not doing anything. . . . I mean if any other kid was invited to a club at 16 and they could get in, they could go too!"[20] Even as an adult, she says, she still frequently checks in with her parents, sometimes calling Kathy as much as five times a day.

Kathy and Rick stood by their daughters as well. Kathy even went so far as to rationalize Paris's skimpy attire at a nightclub as part of a lingerie party: "I know exactly the outfit. . . . It wasn't a G-string! Paris is a most modest girl!"[21]

And there were outsiders who also defended the family. When Paris and Nicky first burst onto the scene, "everyone was like . . . what kind of parents would allow their daughter. . . ." observed social critic and gossip columnist Michael Musto. But at 19 when the *Vanity Fair* piece came out, Paris was "of age to be her own person, and to be acting out in public if she wanted to. And now it's looking like maybe her parents aren't so dumb after all. . . . They've created a superstar." A lot of the animosity toward her on the Internet and elsewhere, Musto believes, is simple jealousy. "She has everything . . . and [some people] hate that kind of person."[22]

Even Francesca Hilton, who today is a comedienne in LA, qualified her censure of her great-niece. "I feel for Paris. She's trying to get attention. She has always been nice, but she is wayward."[23]

THE LESS-THAN-SIMPLE LIFE

Praise her or condemn her, mostly everyone admits that Paris is a good sport, especially at the beginning of her career. Of the teen-aged Paris, Tina Diname of *Star* magazine observed, "Paris loves the spotlight and the spotlight loves Paris. When they ask her for a photograph, she's like, 'Why, sure!' She'll stand there for 20 minutes" until they get the perfect shot.[24] Of course, like many people who have been famous for more than 15 minutes, Paris would eventually develop a love-hate relationship with what she calls the "paps" (short for paparazzi).

Paris has always maintained a sense of humor, even when falling down the stairs at a club in full view of the guests (attributing it to her six-inch heels) or stepping into a blossom-covered pond at a Hollywood party while chatting on the phone (she thought the flowers were decorations for the floor). "An entrance is everything," she has noted, even if it's a pratfall. With a few X-rated and jail-time exceptions, she generally takes what happens to her with a grain of salt. "When you're in an embarrassing situation, just laugh at yourself. If you get embarrassed it will only make the situation worse. Anyway, nobody can hate someone who's laughing at herself."[25] She's game to try anything, whether it's clumsily attempting to operate farm equipment during *The Simple Life* or being thrown from a horse and actually injuring herself during the show's second season.

But *The Simple Life* and its subsequent success didn't just happen; Paris did a lot of groundwork, including modeling as well as television, movie, and other appearances, not to mention attending all those exhausting parties and social events thrown by fellow celebs and wannabes. Her mug popped up on magazines ranging from *Vogue* to *Harper's* to *People* to *InStyle* as well as supermarket tabloids, where she shared headlines with "Satan's Cell Phone Ruined My Life!" "Dog Blows Up Owner!" "Ancient Parking Lot Found on Mars!" and "Exorcists Battle Demon Toupee!" She appeared on awards shows, talk shows, and in music videos with Eminem and Fat Boy Slim and in commercials for T-Mobile and Carl's Hamburgers, among others. She would have probably shown up for the opening of a paper bag if it would have promoted her image.

Even though she didn't really need the money and people with far less income have jobs that require a lot less effort, "I found out I liked working," she said. "It makes you appreciate things more. So, even if people say I'm spoiled at least they can't say I don't do anything. Now I have an agenda like everybody else."[26] And rather than hawk someone else's product as a so-called "heiress PR chick," she took the initiative and began to establish her own brand, which would branch out from acting, modeling, and singing to include jewelry, clothing, handbag design, shoes, and perfume and even a stab at club ownership.

Nicky would develop her own line of apparel as well, attending but not graduating from the Fashion Institute of Technology and Parsons School of Design, both in New York City. Nicky, who had been designing handbags since age 17, launched Chick, her own inexpensive sportswear clothing line for girls and women, in 2004; and three years later, Nicholai, a high-end, luxury apparel line. She has also done some modeling, including runway shows for various designers, and along with childhood friend Kimberly Stewart (daughter of Rod) served as the face of Antz Pantz, the Australian lingerie line. In 2006, and in keeping with family tradition, Nicky planned the opening of her very first Nicky O Hotel in South Beach, 94 condo-type suites to be stylishly furnished and designed by the likes of Roberto Cavalli, Nicole Miller, Heatherette, and Betsey Johnson. However, the venture never got off the ground and she ended up being sued by a business partner.

Even more so than Nicky, Paris was all over the place. Along with *Zoolander* (2001), she did cameos in movies like *The Cat in the Hat* and *Wonderland* (both 2003) and *Raising Helen* (2004). Her first real chance to showcase her acting ability came when she was cast as a jet-setting socialite in the *Nine Lives*. In this 2002 British thriller, several friends reunite for a birthday party on an estate in the isolated, wintry Scottish Highlands. Not surprisingly, uninvited guests drop by and start to kill the buzz and the guests. Paris lasts about 20 minutes or so;

more than one fan and amateur reviewer has commented that the plot died as soon as she did. While in London, she invested in The Collection, an exclusive London eatery with Ivanka Trump (daughter of The Donald) and in 2005 launched the Club Paris nightclub chain in Orlando and Jacksonville, Florida. Although the plan was to expand to other major cities as well as overseas, the original clubs are now defunct.

While Paris was praised as being professional by *Nine Lives* producer Giles Hattersley, making all her early-morning film calls and being pleasant and easy to work with, she was still in her party-hearty phase. She stayed with Hattersley during the several weeks it took to film her part. "She filled our spare room with Gina Shoes, Juicy tracksuits and . . . Guerlain perfume," he observed. It was like having Houseguest Barbie "albeit one with a taste for hard liquor and dubious men. The partying was wild. . . . Everything was pink."

That same year, 2002, was her 21st birthday, and like many people reaching that milestone, she wanted to celebrate. But of course she did it in such a way that the world—and especially the paps—would have to sit up and take notice. So she had five parties in as many different cities, a major media event that required the use of her modeling agency to organize the logistics. The parties were supposed to take place over the period that covered her February 17 birthday, an interval actually longer than 24 hours, considering the time changes in the various continents. Each bash reportedly cost $75,000.

The festivities started out in the Big Apple, in the club room above Studio 54, where mom Kathy had celebrated her own 21st years before. Family and friends only were invited to the ritzy, catered gala decorated with oversize pink and purple feathers, posters of Paris with her then-boyfriend, 28-year-old Tommy Hilfiger model Jason Shaw, and 21 birthday cakes prepared by Le Cirque. There was also a slideshow of Paris's life so far. Finally "legal," Paris drank a glass of champagne, although it was hardly her first. This was followed an undoubtedly wilder but less formal late-night celebration with her peers at the Manhattan club Eugene's.

The other four parties were in LA, Tokyo, London, and Las Vegas. Paris noted that she had friends in all these places, not to mention the jet-setting mix of celebrities and "kids of" such as Enrique Iglesias,

Sarah Gellar, Freddie Prinze Jr., Tara Reid, Pink, and P. Diddy, who were game to celebrate her birthday more than once. And of course she had no choice but to purchase five different outfits along with as many ornate cakes and elaborate decorations, topping it all off with her trademark tiara. "I love tiaras," Paris has observed. "People act differently toward you when you've got jewelry on your head. Especially when they suspect it might be real."[27]

The year 2002 proved to be a landmark juncture for Paris in other ways. That year, Fox TV producer Brad Johnson was casting about for a funny wrinkle in the new but extremely popular reality-TV genre. "The areas that seemed simplest and cleanest was to go back to those high-concept sixties sitcoms and . . . do them for real," he explained.[28] He lit upon a show based upon *Green Acres*, a classic fish-out-of-water comedy featuring Eddie Albert as a former New York lawyer living out his retirement dream as a farmer in Hooterville, USA, and his long-suffering socialite Hungarian wife, played by none other than Eva Gabor, sister of Conrad's second wife Zsa Zsa (proving that even Hollywood can be a small town). The series, which centered on the wealthy city couple's zany adaptation to the rural world, was a huge hit and ran from 1965 to 1971.

Enamored with the notion of a reality show focusing on rich socialites in the middle of nowhere, Johnson was stymied as to who might exactly fit the bill. So he met with the casting department at Fox and Paris's name came up, as someone who was sweet, genuine, and slightly off-kilter; someone who, as one Fox executive observed, was not afraid to traipse through cow patties in her stilettos.

Paris, however, was less enthusiastic about the idea, especially at first. "My mom thought the whole . . . concept was just trying to make fun of me—a couple of rich girls doing gross jobs on a farm—and I know she was probably right." However, the producers begged her, and she relented. "Even to an heiress that's fairly flattering. Particularly to an heiress."[29]

Initially the producers wanted Nicky as the sidekick, but she turned them down flat. She'd had enough of the film industry, although the sisters had cameos in the 2003 film *Pauly Shore Is Dead*, which featured celebrities ranging from Whoopi Goldberg to Sean Penn to Jerry

Springer. "I'm concentrating on fashion," Nicky said. "I have no aspirations to be a singer or actor. Fashion is my priority. I get my inspiration from my hobbies and passions" ranging from horseback riding to (but of course) jewelry to vintage clothing.[30]

Paris agreed that Nicky made the right decision regarding the TV show, given her sister's more reserved nature. So after considering pals Bijou Phillips, Casey Johnson—who would die in January 2010—and Kimberly Stewart, Paris settled on her childhood partner-in-crime Nicole Richie, who had her own baggage; specifically, drug addiction. "I got so much so fast that nothing really excited me anymore," Nicole explained after the fact during a 2007 interview with Diane Sawyer. "I kind of took matters into my own hands and was creating drama in a very dangerous way. I think I was just bored, and I had seen everything—especially when you're young, you just want more."[31]

"I was about 13 when I started drinking," she continued. "I think I started using drugs at 13 as well—smoking pot, cocaine. I would just do a lot of drinking and hang out until six in the morning."[32] By the time she was 18, Nicole had a nasty cocaine habit, and she had graduated to heroin by the time she reached her early twenties.[33]

Although initially she blamed her so-called happy childhood and being spoiled by adoptive dad Lionel Richie, later she owned up to the fact that she had caused her own private hell. "I, again, made the decision for myself, this is something I have to do. I have to get off drugs. This isn't the life . . . this was heroin."[34] Ten days after leaving the Sierra Tucson drug rehab center in Arizona, she and Paris began filming the TV show.

But like her BFF, Nicole was always up for an adventure and didn't seem to care whether people made fun of them or not. "Hopefully they'll be laughing with us," she remarked. "But if not, they'll be laughing anyway."[35] The ultimate goal of course was that both Fox and the girls would be yukking it up all the way to the bank.

While Nicky took the behind-the-scenes road, Paris's decision to go the full exposure route would prove costly and tragic, both personally and professionally. And Nicole was headed right along with her, although her bumpy ride would be quite different from Paris's.

NOTES

1. Paris Hilton with Merle Ginsberg, *Confessions of an Heiress* (New York: Fireside, 2005), 28.

2. Laura Brown, "Partners in Crime," *Harper's Bazaar* 3547 (June 2007): 134.

3. Ibid.

4. Nancy Jo Sales, "Hip Hop Debs," *Vanity Fair* (Sept. 2000): 379.

5. Chas Newkey-Burden, *Paris Hilton: Life on the Edge* (London: John Blake, 2007), 22.

6. Ibid., 34.

7. Sales, "Hip Hop Debs," 378.

8. "The Face of Page Six" (July 21, 2009), www.manhattanmedica.com/pagesix.php.

9. Sales, "Hip Hop Debs," 356.

10. *Paris, Not France*, directed by Adria Petty, documentary (New York: MTV, 2008), unpublished transcript.

11. Newkey-Burden, *Paris Hilton*, 43.

12. Hilton and Ginsberg, *Heiress*, 16.

13. Newkey-Burden, *Paris Hilton*, 22–23.

14. Booth Moore and Renee Tawa, "Paris in the Fall," *Los Angeles Times* (Nov. 18, 2003): E1.

15. Hilton and Ginsberg, *Heiress*, 49.

16. "Wide World of the Wacky Hilton Sibs," *New York Post* (Jan. 13, 2001): 8.

17. Barry Wigmore, "Sister Act," *Mail on Sunday* (London) (Dec. 10, 2000): 40.

18. Newkey-Burden, *Paris Hilton*, 25.

19. Jerry Oppenheimer, *House of Hilton* (New York: Random House, 2006), 258.

20. *Paris, Not France*.

21. Sales, "Hip Hop Debs," 379.

22. *Paris, Not France*.

23. Wigmore, "Sister Act," 40.

24. Newkey-Burden, *Paris Hilton*, 35–36.

25. Hilton and Ginsberg, *Heiress*, 87.

26. Ibid., 101.

27. Ibid., 7.

28. Newkey-Burden, *Paris Hilton*, 81.

29. Hilton and Ginsberg, *Heiress*, 112.

30. Cathy Rose A. Garcia, "Nicky Hilton Serious about Fashion," *Korean Times* (May 23, 2008), www.koreatimes.co.kr/www/news/art/2009/09/199_24642.html.

31. Stephen M. Silverman, "Nicole Richie: Boredom Led to Drug Use," People.com (Aug. 4, 2007), www.people.com/people/article/0,,20050008,00.html.

32. "Happiness Drove Nicole Richie to Drugs" (March 28, 2006), socialitelife.celebuzz.com/archive/2006/03/28/happiness_drove_nicole_richie_to_drugs.php.

33. Ibid.

34. Ibid.

35. Newkey-Burden, *Paris Hilton*, 83.

Chapter 4

BAD DECISIONS, OVEREXPOSURE, AND EMBARRASSING MOMENTS

At the beginning of and throughout her career, Paris has had her share of detractors and has often been slammed as being "famous for being famous," a "celebutard," and an "heirhead." In a poll conducted by the Associated Press and AOL, Paris was voted the second-worst celebrity role model of 2006, behind Britney Spears. Along with being designated as the most overrated celebrity by the *Guinness Book of World Records* in 2007, she was part of an experiment that February by the Associated Press *not* to report on her activities for a week, an attempt that obviously backfired.

However, the other side of the coin glimmered with praise, in spite of the infamous sex tape. In 2004, a few months after the tape was released, Paris was named one of the "10 Most Fascinating People" in a Barbara Walters TV special. That same year she was also deemed a top-10 celebrity by *Rolling Stone* magazine. "She's an American sphinx with no secrets, always tilting her head for the camera at that same eerie angle, always flashing that same eerie smile," cooed the magazine. "We have no idea where this girl is going, but we have the strangest feeling we are going there with her."[1] Paris is also credited with popularizing the expression "That's hot!" although some sources claim

that the phrase originated in black urban areas and Paris picked it up
through her association with hip-hop record producer Damon Dash
and rapper Jay-Z.[2] Numerous appearances on national talk shows ranging from David Letterman to Ellen DeGeneres as well as *Saturday Night
Live* also did much to raise her visibility.

GIRL ON FILM

And along with the success of *The Simple Life*—the premiere episode drew 13 million viewers, increasing Fox's 18–49 viewer share to
79 percent—Paris began to garner major film roles. In 2005, she was
melting hearts and skin as Paige Edwards in the thriller *House of Wax*, a
remake of the classic 1953 Vincent Price creeper that revolves around
a ghoulish wax museum. In the updated version, six teenagers on their
way to a football game decide to set up camp for the night and are
visited by a stranger in a pickup truck who refuses to leave until one of
the boys smashes a headlight with a bottle. Not surprisingly, the next
morning, the kids' car has become inoperable, leaving them in the
hands of a creepy rural man named Lester, who takes them to a town—
ostensibly to get a fan belt—whose main attraction is a wax museum.
One by one the teenagers realize that the entire town is nothing but
dead citizens who have become embalmed as realistic-looking wax figures, and soon all but two, including Paris, join the population. Nick
and Carly, a brother and sister and the only teens to remain alive, set
fire in the building's basement to stop their attackers. The fire spreads
through the museum, and the teens kill the museum owners—who are
also siblings—and escape as the building melts to the ground.

In 2006, Paris had the lead and was executive producer of *National
Lampoon's Pledge This!* a straight-to-DVD film about a goofy sorority;
Nicky also had an uncredited appearance. When a dorm toilet ex-
plodes on their first day back at college, a group of misfit girlfriends are
forced to search for a new residence. The girls decide to pledge Gamma
Gamma, the most exclusive sorority at South Beach University, led by
president Victoria English, played by Paris. Victoria/Paris only allows
them entry to display diversity, a requirement to win the "Hottest Sorority in the Country" contest held by a popular men's magazine. But
once Gloria, one of the girls, catches the eye of Victoria's boyfriend

Paris Hilton poses during a photo call for her film Pledge This! *directed by William Heins, at the 58th International Cannes Film Festival in Cannes, southern France, May 13, 2005. (AP Photo/ Michel Euler)*

Derek, all Hell Week breaks loose, and although they are pledged, Victoria kicks them out after Gamma Gamma wins the contest. In a case of life imitating art, the misfit freshmen sneak back into the sorority house and steal embarrassing photos and video footage of Victoria to show to everyone at the Gamma Gamma victory party. Gloria also reveals that she and Derek love each other. A humbled and embarrassed Victoria makes a public apology to the freshmen, and Gloria becomes the president of the sorority the following year (apparently she had been reinstated off-camera).

In 2008 Paris also starred in *The Hottie and the Nottie* about Nate, a geeky guy with a fantasy crush on Cristabel (Paris), his grade school girlfriend. Nate sets out for California to hunt down Cristabel, who jogs on the beach every day with many suitors trying to catch her eye. While Cristabel is still single, it's because she's remained best friends with a homely girl with the unfortunate and very un-PC name of June Phigg, who Nate also knew in first grade. According to the entertainment Web site glam.com:

Nate reintroduces himself to Cristabel and they hit it off. However, Cristabel refuses to go on a date with Nate unless June has a date as well. Nate sets out to find a boyfriend for June, but guys recoil at the sight of her. At the Santa Monica Pier, Johann, an attractive dentist who works as a part-time model, appears in their lives. He seems to want to do a makeover on June. As Nate and June become friends and she emerges from her cocoon, Nate slowly realizes that she may be the girl of his dreams.[3]

While the movies made money, especially overseas, they and often Paris in particular were mostly panned by critics and some viewers. Paris had the dubious honor of receiving the "Worst Actress" Golden Raspberry ("Razzie") awards for both *House of Wax* and *The Hottie and the Nottie*. Considered the foremost authority on big-screen stinkers, the Razzies serve as a counterpoint to the Oscars, are announced around the same time, and get a great deal of press coverage. However, Paris did garner some kudos, in particular Teen Choice Awards for "Best Scream" and "Female Breakout Performance" for her work in *House of Wax*.

FROM X-RATED . . .

Unfortunately Paris was to get another honor, one she would have preferred not to. That would be Adult Video News (AVN) Award for best renting and selling title of 2005 for "1 Night in Paris," a homemade sex tape produced and directed a year earlier by ex-boyfriend Rick Salomon. Until the premiere of *The Simple Life*, Paris might have agreed with the concept that there's no such thing as bad publicity. But a few days before the show's premiere on December 2, 2003, a shorter version of the video was leaked onto the Internet and immediately became viral, proliferating everywhere. Paris was so devastated that she went into hiding and refused to do promotion for the TV show.

The film was shot in grainy detail, showing what appears to be a somewhat out-of-it Paris with Salomon; at one point she even interrupted the proceedings to answer her ringing cell phone. Even years later she recalls finding out about the tape in horror:

I don't remember filming it in the first place. I didn't even know there was [a tape]. I saw it online . . . and completely broke down. I could not believe what I was seeing. . . . It's the most intimate thing you can do and the whole [bleeping] world is laughing at you.[4]

Paris also claims to have been younger than 19, the age Salomon declared she was when he filmed her, although he lasciviously kept referring to her extreme youth throughout the tape. Almost equally upsetting to her was that Salomon violated her trust. The relationship "didn't end badly, I just didn't want to talk to him anymore. I had a new boyfriend and a new life." She called Salomon and begged him not to release the DVD, although her pleas fell on deaf ears. "My friends told me [years ago] he said he knew I was going to be famous and he was going to film it and make a lot of money."[5]

A self-admitted drug dealer, Richard Allan Salomon is the son of a former Warner Bros. executive vice president. He moved from New Jersey to Hollywood in the early 1980s, quickly hooking up with a fast crowd and living the high life thanks to the lucrative drug trade. His main talent seemed to be marrying and divorcing famous women: voice-over actress Elizabeth Daily (1995–2000); Shannen Doherty of *Beverly Hills 90210* (2002–3); and *Baywatch* babe and supermodel Pamela Anderson (2007–8), not to mention liaisons with Paris, Drew Barrymore, and other assorted models and Playmates. He seems continually mired in controversy and sleazy deals, including lawsuits and countersuits with the Hilton family over publication of the "1 Night in Paris" videotape as well as with Anderson over the validity of their marriage.[6]

The media furor over the sex tape was so intense that it even eclipsed the war in Iraq, which in late 2003 was only a few months old. Even the *New York Times* did a satire on a videotaped "encounter" between Paris and a mathematician at Princeton in which they discuss developing a low-cost irrigation system to help starving countries, also with a scene involving a ringing cell phone. Unlike the original, Paris is apparently so involved in the conversation that she deigns not to answer it.

And even those with little room to talk offered an opinion: "I don't think it's that damaging in the long term," observed fellow daughter of

privilege, publicist Lizzie Grubman, whose father is entertainment lawyer Allen Grubman. Paris "does have a show to promote, and I think it
will help sell the show."[7] Hardly a model of discretion herself, in 2001
a drunk Grubman backed her SUV into a crowd of people outside a
club in the Hamptons, injuring 16. The felony should have earned her
eight years in prison, but her high-powered attorney got her off with
37 days in jail and five years probation. Quite a contrast from Paris's
23 days in lockup for driving under the influence with a suspended
license in 2007.

Naturally, Rick and Kathy were appalled by the video. They issued
a public statement of support for their daughter, although things were
not so calm privately: Kathy sought the help of a therapist, and Rick
later admitted that it was probably one of the most stressful situations
the family had ever endured. Along with threatening to sue Salomon,
the Hiltons brought out the big guns: specifically, public relations guru
Dan Klores, who was known as a pit bull when it came to damage
control. He'd handled troublesome situations and litigation for Mike
Tyson, Donald Trump, the late Michael Jackson, and others.

Rather than make a big deal of it, Klores downplayed the entire affair as a lousy example of not-so-great sex during a grim time when the
public was looking for any diversion. He adhered to Paris's wishes for
no interviews, with one notable exception: a clever skit on *Saturday
Night Live* with comedian Jimmy Fallon, full of double entendres and
innuendoes in which Paris poked fun at the tape and herself. It went a
long way toward putting the situation into its proper perspective.

"From the start the only thing I was gonna let [Paris] do was, 'Saturday Night Live,'" Klores recalled. And even though she was scared and
intimidated by not only him but the whole dilemma, he admired her
gumption. "She was very disciplined; she came to New York [for the
show] and didn't go anywhere" else.[8]

Despite attempted legal action by the Hilton family to stop its publication, a 60-minute version of the sex tape was later released in DVD
format in 2004. To protect his so-called reputation, Salomon filed a
countersuit against the Hiltons, asserting that they tried to portray him
as a rapist, which of course the family denied. The Hiltons and Salomon settled out of court for what some sources estimate to be about
$400,000. However, Paris claimed never to have received a dime. "It's

just dirty money and he [Salomon] should give it all to some charity for the sexually abused or something."[9] Ironically, Salomon's company, Red Light District Video, dedicated the video "in memory of 9/11/01."

Soon afterward, things settled down somewhat. In a public statement, Kathy remarked that the family's love and support for each other helped them get through this crisis. "It wasn't [Paris's] fault; a lot of young people take these sort of pictures. You think you are in love with a boy, decide to do a video and, all of a sudden, it gets into the wrong hands." Of course, being a mother she added, "It wasn't the sort of thing we'd do, but today is a different day and age."[10]

And for Paris, time has provided some much-needed perspective. "It's, like, everyone has sex," she recently observed. "It's not like it was [with] some random person."[11]

TO EXCELLENT RATINGS

And Paris had a show to contend with, one that by all accounts was shaping up to be a major hit. As is often the case with something that skirts the edges of good taste and popular culture, the critics weren't always kind: "The rich are very different from you and me," one sniped. "They're morons."[12] Added another: "What do you get when you combine incredibly rich with incredibly dumb? Paris and Nicole's big adventure, that's what!"[13] Others, however, saw it as a hilarious treatise on present-day society: "Leave it to others to comment on the meaning of all this," remarked Jonathan Storm from the *Philadelphia Inquirer*. "I'm too busy laughing my pants off."[14] The show ran for five seasons.

And the public ate it up, especially the 18–49 male demographic. In the premiere, after an elaborate going-away party at the Hilton mansion, the girls were swept away (by private jet of course) into the wilds of Altus, Arkansas, population 817. They were to live with a family of seven, the Ledings, in an unfinished room that was actually a back porch covering a well.

They freaked out over sharing a bathroom, plucking a chicken, and an enormous tick in their bedroom, flirting outrageously with the family's naïve teenaged son. At dinner, Paris came forth with one of her famous malapropisms, asking if they actually sold walls at Wal-Mart—a store she claimed to have never heard of—while Nicole wondered what a soup kitchen was after they went over budget and the snippy cashier informed them that the grocery store they were shopping in definitely was not one. Subsequent episodes (Dec. 2003–Jan. 2004) saw them crashing and burning at jobs ranging from burger flippers to dairy farm workers to gas station attendants, among other things.

However, while she and Nicole may have been uneducated about farming and chores pertaining to earning minimum wage, "we weren't as naïve as they portrayed us on the show," remarked Paris, adding that it would not have been nearly been as funny had they not hammed it up. Plus, "we really did do all those gross things. There were no body doubles."[15]

In season two (June–Aug. 2004) the girls and their pets traversed the South in a pink pickup and bunked in an attached Airstream trailer. They stayed with several hosting families, including hippies, bikers, and Fundamentalists. With no money, credit cards or cell phones, they also had to work various jobs in order to survive. During the premiere, Paris was thrown from a horse while herding bulls on a ranch in Florida. She blamed it on the cameras, which were scaring the horses: "I went flying into the air and actually fell under the horse," she recalled. Its hooves went into her, "and it galloped right on top of me!" Although she seemed unharmed except for a few bruises—the crew kept on filming throughout the accident—as a precaution the Fox producers had her airlifted to a Tampa hospital where she checked out fine. However, she found the experience traumatic: "I don't know if I'll even be able to watch the [episode], let alone get on another horse."[16]

The rest of the season offered more comedy than drama: Paris and Nicole as mermaids in an underwater show, as—Eeuuww!—sausage makers and craw fishers—and as deputy sheriffs, feeding prisoners and issuing tickets. They were also employed by a baseball team, in a beauty salon, and perhaps most intriguingly as maids in a nudist resort, where they partied at a nude disco once they were off the clock. Paris was flummoxed by all the exposed body parts and the fact that most of the residents were closer to their parents' age. "And people accuse me of being an exhibitionist! I was the person with the most clothes on in the room!"[17]

While being reality TV stars may seem glamorous to the viewer, in truth it was often exhausting, uncomfortable, and a lot of hard work.

The girls shared a bed and had to deal with bugs constantly swarming around the camera lights, not to mention the growing pile of dirty clothes and messes from their respective pets. Because they had no money, they sometimes had to beg people to pay for their food or ask for free handouts from restaurants. The bolder and more outspoken of the duo, Nicole seemed unfazed by requesting freebies, while Paris was content to stand there, look "hot," and smile.

Season three (Jan.–May 2005) turned up the heat on the girls even more. Not only did they serve as interns staying with 15 different families, but they traveled the East Coast with at least some of the great unwashed public on a Greyhound bus. Their gamut of duties ranged from day care to working in a mortuary to assisting a plastic surgeon, the latter of which completely grossed them out. They also served as firefighters, in a manufacturing facility where they caused double trouble with bubble wrap (a la Lucy and Ethel in the famous *I Love Lucy* candy factory episode), and in a dentist's office, where they were supposed to drill but ended up insulting patients and putting makeup on them instead. They also involved their host families in their adventures—attending a transvestite show, taking judo lessons, and entering a beauty pageant.

FROM BESTIES TO BREAKUP AND BACK AGAIN

By season four (June–Aug. 2006), however, Fox was ready to give up the show, the official reason being that they had no room on their schedule. And Paris and Nicole were no longer on speaking terms, a rift that allegedly occurred months before filming was to begin.

The reasons for the girls' breakup were subject to wild speculation. Paris commented, "It's no big secret that Nicole and I are no longer friends. Nicole knows what she did, and that's all I'm ever going to say about it."[18] Neither young woman ever spoke publicly about the cause of the split, though rumors suggested that the pair fell out due to Nicole "accidentally" showing the "1 Night in Paris" sex tape to a group of their friends who were gathered at sister Nicky's home. Paris allegedly ran from the house in tears.

Nicole's official stance was that they had simply grown apart; she denied ever showing the tape. "I'm sure it stirs up controversy, which I'm sure that Paris loves but I really have nothing bad to say about her."[19]

But as mentioned earlier, Hollywood can be a small town, and the girls endured awkward moments when out and about—showing up the same time at the Hyde Lounge; bumping into each other in the green room at MTV's Video Music Awards; and ignoring each other while gossip swirled around them, such as the rumor that Paris was making prank phone calls to Nicole at all hours of the night. If one were to believe the Hollywood rumor mill, it would seem that both women were in junior high and not in their mid-twenties.

But *The Simple Life* was not destined to be orphaned for long. Lured by high ratings, the E! Entertainment network quickly picked up season four. Here the girls were to play "wife" and stay in LA with several families, in a format similar to the TV show *Wife Swap*. Along with keeping their cell phones and credit cards, they also had various well-known family members, friends, and associates as guests in several episodes. The producers got around the feud by having them film separately and alternating between the family during each episode. The twist was that the families got to decide which girl was better in the role of wife/mother.

In the premiere, each strapped on a 35-pound pregnancy suit, cleaned house, wrangled with a three-year-old, and attended Lamaze class. Nicole took the dad to a strip club, so predictably the nine-months-pregnant wife chose Paris as the "winner." Paris's prize was to witness a videotape of the birth, which grossed her out so much that she threw up. During the rest of the season, the girls individually took over the responsibilities of a traditional Pakistani mother, struggled with four out-of-control kids, and planned a birthday party and a camping trip, among other things.

A confrontation was orchestrated during the finale, when a Paris look-alike and Nicole ended up at the home at the same time. Nicole retaliated by calling a press conference, which Paris got wind of. The cliffhanger ending resulted in Paris confronting Nicole, stating, "We have to talk," and followed by a screen that read "To be continued . . . next season!"

Actually, the girls had already begun to reconcile, officially mending fences on Nicole's birthday late in September 2006 at a very public meeting at the Beverly Hills Hotel, where, followed by a mass of buzzing paps, they repaired to dad Lionel's house for a long heart-to-heart.

A few days later, they were also spotted having dinner at Dan Tana's Steakhouse in West Hollywood. Paris recalled:

> There was no reason why we were fighting; it was just silly. We believed what other people were saying. People are really two-faced in this town, and they were trying to play us against each other. It made me sadder than any breakup with a boyfriend. It was just like the worst feeling ever.[20]

They have remained friends, although not quite the inseparable "besties," of the first few seasons. But each seemed to come away with an increased appreciation for the other, especially in contrast with other female celebrity peers, such as Paris's confrontations with actress Lindsay Lohan and Nicole's fashionista altercations with her former stylist Rachel Zoe.

Nicole's bouts with weight issues—she denied being anorexic or bulimic but was in treatment several times for excessive weight loss and dehydration—and both girls' subsequent DUI (driving under the influence) run-ins with the law resulted in filming delays for season five, *The Simple Life Goes to Camp* (May–Aug. 2007). The season picked up where the last left off, with Paris and Nicole recreating their true-to-life reconciliation onscreen for viewers and then being driven by limo to the campsite. The girls were to work with various celebrities as well as the campers for Wellness Camp, Pageant Camp, Couples Camp, Survival Camp, and Drama Camp.

However, while it's largely understood that certain aspects of reality shows are scripted with confrontations or other drama engineered for viewers' entertainment, they are supposed to be based on real people and places. And although Paris and Nicole were roughing it as counselors, "Camp Shawnee" in Malibu wasn't exactly kosher, although it was in actuality a camp for Jewish youth, JCA Shalom. The alleged "directors" weren't even listed on the camp's Web page, and "counselor" Hunter Cross, Paris's romantic interest during the show, turned out to be an aspiring actor and former Abercrombie & Fitch model. Even the camp "nurse" was listed as an actress on the Internet Movie Database (IMDB), and although most of the campers were nonactors at least one had been spotted on a commercial. Observed E!Insider: "The only 'real' people from Camp JCA Shalom to appear on the show are Jorge, the camp chef, and Julia, the camp dog."[21]

The audience apparently picked up on the lack of authenticity. Although season four was a hit by E! standards, drawing nearly one million viewers per episode, season five saw a sharp decline in ratings. By the seventh episode, the ratings had dropped to around 700,000 viewers. So on July 30, 2007, E! announced that the show would not be renewed for a sixth season. Paris and Nicole, it seemed, were ready to move onto other pastures, some greener, others not so much.

Like Paris, Nicole has pursued several different careers. She joined a rock band, acted in the 2004 movie *Kids in America*, and even authored a semi-biographical 2005 novel, *The Truth about Diamonds*, which sold surprisingly well. After the show's cancellation, she debuted a jewelry line and designed maternity clothes, in addition to starting a charitable foundation for children with her partner, Joel Madden. And like Paris and her sister Nicky, she was considered a style icon, appearing on many best-dressed lists. Her dramatic weight loss was subject to endless speculation, although in 2006 she remarked, "I know I'm too thin right now, so I wouldn't want any young girl looking at me and saying, 'That's what I want to look like.'"[22]

But unlike her former BFF, Nicole's romantic relationships have been fewer and longer-lasting. For two years, she dated the late Adam Goldstein, also known as club disc jockey DJ AM, who died of an accidental drug overdose in August 2009 at age 36. They were engaged for nine months, splitting in 2006. Shortly afterward she became involved with her current partner, guitarist Joel Madden of the band Good Charlotte. (Paris also dated his identical twin brother and fellow band member, guitarist Benji Madden, for a few months in 2008, even announcing her hopes to marry him during an interview with talk show host David Letterman.)

So far the Nicole/Joel Madden pairing has produced two offspring: daughter Harlow Winter Kate Madden on January 11, 2008, and some 21 months later, son Sparrow James Midnight Richie Madden on September 9, 2009. Nicole and her live-in seem to have cornered the market on inventive names, even inspiring the Hollywood Web site Gawker.com to try to one-up them with suggestions such as Old Latrobe Kardashian, Dodo Centrifuge Simpson-Wentz, Michelin Sapphire Klum, Chinoiserie Dymphna Jolie-Pitt, Hardy Henson Affleck, and Revenge Validation Aniston, among others.[23] And the couple plan to expand their family. "I want five children," Nicole said. "Twin boys and three girls. I've wanted that since I was a little girl."[24]

Following Paris's example, in February 2010, Nicole announced her engagement to Joel, also on *The Late Show with David Letterman*. Nicole's proclamation seems more durable than her former BFF's, as she and Joel had made the decision to wed several months before and it had been somewhat of an open secret among family and close friends, Joel having tweeted to his followers that they were "all good tight lipped people who let us enjoy it!" However, as of this writing, no official wedding date has been set.

THE SIMPLE LIFE: CANINE VERSION

There was a third star on *The Simple Life*—one who accompanied Paris through all five seasons—and who never had a bad word to say about anyone. That would be man's, or in this case, woman's, best friend, her beloved Chihuahua Tinkerbell. "Tink," as she's affectionately called, was purchased in 2002 from Texas Teacups, an online breeder. The privileged pooch arrived on a plane, as was fitting for an heiress's dog.

Although Paris has owned a menagerie of pets, from small dogs to purebred kittens to a mini-pig to ferrets, she and Tinkerbell have a special bond; and in fact the little Chihuahua has accompanied her everywhere, to the point that she (Tink) was dubbed an "accessory dog." "Tink and I are a lot alike," Paris noted. "I'm her stylist and I can tell you she dresses really cute!"[25] Outfits included a little pink and white designer coat with cherries on it and color-coordinated booties, accented by a Swarovski crystal collar/leash combo. Of course, Tink also had her nails painted to match.

In fact, Tinkerbell had become so popular that she "authored" a memoir, *The Tinkerbell Hilton Diaries: My Life Tailing Paris Hilton*, in 2004, which had originally started out as a blog on the Internet. Tink's biting observations, channeled through human humorist D. Resin, ranged from "Oh, for the love of God . . . I'm in a pink angora sweater. I would try to kick my own ass if I met me" to complaints about having to smell "heiress armpit" all day long.[26] Although not exactly Virginia

Paris Hilton, hotel heiress and star of the reality television show The Simple Life, *holds her pet Chihuahua, Tinkerbell, at a Miami Beach hotel, March 11, 2004. (AP Photo/ Bill Cooke)*

Woof—er Woolf—Tink/D. Resin chronicled the angst of life in the Paris lane, from annoyance at being confused with the house Pomeranians to exasperation at her owner's "blonde" moments of trying to recharge cell phone batteries in the microwave and stuffing $100 bills into a vending machine to concern over being paired with a male teacup Chihuahua, who would probably end up being gay so Tink would have to compete with him for the best outfits.

Tink also seemed to share her owner's sense of irony: "I'm one of those dogs . . . that people cheer when a falcon swoops down and disappears into the sky with one in its talons." Of Paris, she somewhat brutally observed, "A mere bitch hasn't had a ride this good since Marie Antoinette before the butler let the mob in."[27] Despite its childlike cover and layout of mostly pictures, *The Tinkerbell Hilton Diaries* was obviously not for kids.

But even the best dog's life has its challenging moments. In August 2004, Tinkerbell disappeared from Paris's LA digs. And possibly even worse, she (Tink) was naked. After a few days of anonymously posting pictures of a "lost dog" Chihuahua around West Hollywood with offers of a $1,000 reward, Paris finally went public and upped the ante to $5,000 for Tink's safe return. She was reluctant to openly admit that the missing pooch was Tinkerbell, expressing the fear that the ransom might go to the millions of dollars.

However, Tink was found 6 days later, under circumstances that were never fully explained. Theories abounded, ranging from a possible treatment at a canine Betty Ford Center (a few days in dog years being approximately equal to 28 human days) to an act of revenge from a jealous ex-boyfriend of Paris's to a publicity stunt for Tink's upcoming diary due to be published in a couple of weeks. Or perhaps sister Nicky simply left the door open to the home she shared with Paris at the time and Tink went out to pick up a few things at the drugstore. Some speculated that Tink fell into Ugg boot, only to be located after an exhaustive search of the house. Given her mistress's penchant for timely publicity, it's a good guess that her dog's vanishing act was just that and Tink never actually left the building.

Regardless, things quickly returned to normal for Tinkerbell, in spite of the addition of several pets. (In her diary, Tink expressed insecurity over her ability to maintain her mistress's affections: "My hide matches suede. . . . If Paris gets bored with me I don't want to end up as a hat or something. If I suddenly start not showing up in pictures . . . please call the police!"[28]) Tinkerbell's worries were unfounded, and she continued to be a lap dog of luxury, in 2009 joining Marilyn Monroe, Dolce, Prada, and two other pooches in a $325,000 custom palace built just for them. The two-floor pink chateau, estimated at around 300 square feet, was a miniature version of Paris's mansion, boasting miniature Philippe Starck furniture, indoor heat and air conditioning, and a crystal chandelier and ceiling moldings. Downstairs was a living room, and the upstairs bedroom boasted a "Furcedes," a bed in the shape in a car and a closet jam-packed with the pets' clothes. However, the house lacked indoor plumbing, and the dogs still did their business outside.

Although she (Paris) was criticized for extravagance at a time when many people were losing their homes to a recession, Paris also donated some of the proceeds from a line of dog clothes that she designed to animal rescue groups. "I like to dress the [dogs], so . . . it's really cute, like dresses and jeans—everything you can imagine for humans, but for dogs," she explained.[29] The Hollywood boutique, Little Lilly, that carried her fashions catered to pampered canines all over the world, from those of the rich and famous to four-legged movie stars to anyone who could afford Paris's mid-priced retail offerings.

And Tink also supposedly has the final yap when it comes to men. "If she likes a guy, I know they're good," Paris observed. "I'd go out with a guy who was really funny and honest—or someone Tinkerbell really liked."[30] Yet considering Paris's romantic history, she hasn't always listened to her animal's instincts and has sometimes even ignored her own.

NOTES

1. Rob Sheffield, Mark Binelli, Greil Marcus, Austin Scaggs, et al., "People of the Year," *Rolling Stone* 964/965 (Dec. 30, 2004–Jan. 13, 2005): 66.

2. Urban Dictionary, "That's Hot!" www.urbandictionary.com/define. php?term=That'shot.

3. "The Hottie and the Nottie," synopsis, glam.com (2008), television.glam.com/topics/detail/noise/video/404495216/.

4. *Paris, Not France*, directed by Adria Petty, documentary (New York: MTV, 2008), unpublished transcript.

5. Ibid.

6. "Pamela Anderson and Rick Salomon: Marriage Annulled!" (March 25, 2008), www.thehollywoodgossip.com/2008/03/pamela-anderson-and-rick-salomon-marriage-annulled/.

7. John Leland, "Once You've Seen Paris Everything Is E = mc2," *New York Times* (Nov. 23, 2003): 9.

8. Chas Newkey-Burden, *Paris Hilton: Life on the Edge* (London: John Blake, 2007), 72–73.

9. "Paris Hilton: I'm Not Having Sex for a Year" (August 6, 2006), www.entertainmentwise.com/news.

10. "Kathy Hilton Defends Paris' Sex Tape Shame" (November 5, 2005), www.contactmusic.com/new/xmlfeed.nsf/story/kathy-hilton-defends-paris-sex-tape-shame.

11. Newkey-Burden, *Paris Hilton*, 75.

12. Mike Argento, "Very Rich, Very Spoiled and Very Stupid," *York* [PA] *Daily Record* (Dec. 8, 2003): 1.

13. Linda Stasi, "Hilton Heads: Rumors of a Raunchy Home Video Gives New Meaning to 'Simple Life,'" *New York Post* (Nov. 10, 2003): 83.

14. Jonathan Storm, "Paris Plays a Clueless Blonde: Herself. Two Heiresses Are Unintentionally Hilarious as They Rough It in Arkansas," *Philadelphia Inquirer* (Nov. 30, 2003): H1.

15. Paris Hilton with Merle Ginsberg, *Confessions of an Heiress* (New York: Fireside, 2005), 113.

16. Ibid., 121.

17. Ibid., 122.

18. "Paris Speaks out about Split with Nicole," People.com (March 21, 2005), www.people.com/people/article/0,,1052425,00.html.

19. "Paris Hilton Suspected to Have Pranked Nicole Richie" (Nov. 11, 2005), news.softpedia.com/news/Paris-Hilton-Suspected-To-Have-Pranked-Nicole-Richie-12240.shtml.

20. Laura Brown, "Partners in Crime," *Harper's Bazaar* 3547 (June 2007): 134.

21. Anonymous blog, the E!Insider online (posted 4/1/08), boards.eonline.com/Insider/Boards/message.jspa?messageID=2120345.

22. Marla Lehner, "Nicole Richie: 'I'm Too Thin,'" People.com (May 4, 2006), www.people.com/people/article/0,,1190900,00.html.

23. Brian Moylan, "After Sparrow Madden What Celebrity Baby Names Are Left?" Gawker.com (Sept. 9, 2009), gawker.com/5355918/after-sparrow-madden-what-celebrity-baby-names-are-left.

24. "Nicole Richie's Domestic Bliss," *Harper's Bazaar* 3559 (June 2008): 172.

25. Hilton and Ginsberg, *Heiress*, 166.

26. Tinkerbell Hilton, *The Tinkerbell Hilton Diaries: My Life Tailing Paris Hilton* (New York: Warner Books, 2004).

27. Ibid.

28. Ibid.

29. Mignon A. Gould, "Paris Talks Togs—People's and Pet's," *Arizona Republic* (Feb. 8, 2008), electronic database access [Proquest].

30. Stephen M. Silverman, "Paris's Dog Tale to Set Tongues Wagging," People.com (Aug. 20, 2004), www.people.com/people/article/0,26334,685414,00.html.

Chapter 5

FACING THE CONSEQUENCES

Nowhere is the rift between rumor and fact more apparent than in love and the law. And Paris has had plenty of encounters with both. The architect of many of her own romantic disasters, she is rarely without a boyfriend, usually a hot, famous actor or heir. She has been engaged several times and has impulsively and publicly declared her intentions to marry several boyfriends, much to her later embarrassment and that of her significant ex.

The same was essentially true of her jail sentence. Despite being pulled over for DWI and reckless driving on three occasions, having her license suspended and being handed a written warning by the officer, Paris continued to do as she pleased, ignoring the ramifications. Like many people who are just starting out, she avoided what she'd rather not deal with. Unfortunately—or perhaps fortunately, considering it turned out to be a major life lesson—Paris ended up in jail for 23 days.

Throughout these difficult times, most of which were in her early to mid-twenties, Paris may have been experiencing what's commonly known as the "quarter-life crisis," when one feels adrift, confused about where to head next and not quite sure which path to take. But since she chose to live in the spotlight, every step and misstep is exposed to its unrelenting glare. And while many, although not all, of her peers make major or similar mistakes and bad decisions, everything Paris Hilton has done and likely will do, whether true or untrue, has become a part of the public record.

THEY LOVE PARIS IN THE SPRING, SUMMER, FALL . . .

Paris has claimed to be very selective about her relationships, pointing out that although she's been linked with several men, that hardly means she's slept with all of them. "People make up stories, but mostly I just kiss," she remarked. "I think it's important to play hard to get. Nobody wants the fake Prada bag; they want the brand new bag that no one can get and is the most expensive. If you give it up to a guy he won't respect you; he'll want you much more if he can't have you."[1]

An attractive and striking young teen, Paris began dating while in junior high. Her first boyfriend "of record" was Randy Spelling, son of the late legendary TV producer Aaron Spelling and brother of actress and reality-TV star Tori. Paris was 15 and Randy 17 when she supposedly lost her virginity to him. "We went to Palm Springs once for the weekend, and we couldn't check into the hotel under her name because her grandma was looking for her," he recalled. "And what do you know, I hear this knock-knock-knock on the door, and I look out and her grandma's there. And then I look out the window and I see Paris in a full-on dress with a suitcase running down the golf course. We broke up like a week later."[2]

According to him, Paris has fond memories of the romance; when he encountered her in an LA nightclub a decade later she came over to greet him. "She was like, 'Randy took my virginity. I want to say hi.'"[3] However, Paris has remained mum regarding this matter.

Paris was around 18 or so when she first became involved with Rick Salomon, although she has often described herself as a "little girl" in reference to the sex tape. According to her, they dated for over three years. "I was in love with that man," she has said.[4]

But she and Salomon drifted apart as she discovered men closer to her age with whom she had more in common. Their star was on the rise, as was hers. Her first engagement was to fashion model Jason Shaw from mid-2002 to early 2003. When Paris met him at age 21, he was in his late twenties, a high-profile model for Tommy Hilfiger, and the object of many girls' fantasies. However, they grew apart as her career began to bloom. "Jason was her first love, her first serious relationship and it was hard for him to be in [Paris's] spotlight," explained Paris's aunt Kyle Richards.[5]

In 2003–4 she had a relationship with singer Nick Carter, who later confessed to sleeping with singer Ashlee Simpson while still involved with Paris. That was followed by pairing of Parises (Parii?), a brief engagement to the Greek shipping heir Paris Latsis, from May–November 2005. Then she began dating another Greek shipping heir, Stavros Niarchos III, before breaking up in May 2006, although she's been out with him several times since and they've been photographed snuggling.

Shortly after the relationship with Niarchos ended, she publicly announced that she was abstaining from sex for a year. She believed that taking a break from boyfriends would help her rediscover herself and define what she really wanted. "Every time I have a boyfriend, I'm just so romantic, and I'll put all my energy into the guy, and I don't really pay attention to myself," she observed. Plus, she added, almost as an afterthought: "Guys want you more if you don't just hand it to them on a platter. If they want you, then they will wait."[6]

So it wasn't until early 2008 that she became involved again, this time with Good Charlotte guitarist Benji Madden, whose twin brother Joel is Nicole Richie's significant other and the father of Nicole's two children. Despite Paris's declared plans to marry Benji during a May interview with late-night talk show host David Letterman, the two ended it in November of that year, although they've supposedly remained friends.

Paris's most recent on-again off-again romance has been with *The Hills* TV show star Doug Reinhardt. They began their tumultuous relationship in February 2009 and then broke up in June, reconciling in August. Although she'd stated that she planned to marry Reinhardt, they had several widely publicized fights along with displays of affection.

In April 2010, Paris ended it with Reinhardt; this time, she said, permanently. "I just realized that I'm better off without him," she

*Paris Hilton, left, and Doug
Reinhardt arrive at the LA Gay
and Lesbian Center "An Evening
with Women" Gala in Beverly
Hills, CA, on April 24, 2009.
(AP Photo/Dan Steinberg)*

remarked. "I deserve something much better. He wasn't right for me
and I will eventually find somebody who loves me for who I am."[7]
Neither wasted time in showing up with someone else: soon after the
breakup, Paris was spotted out to dinner with ex-fiancé Jason Shaw.
And while Reinhardt was reportedly devastated by the split, he was
also photographed at the West Hollywood club with a blonde, 24-year-
old Paris look-alike.

   Paris claimed to enjoy being single again and comforted herself
by purchasing a new pug puppy to add to her canine coterie of her
17 Chihuahuas and one Pomeranian and throwing herself into her
latest projects, cleavage-flattering lingerie and a new album (see chapter 7). But the reprieve from male companionship was short-lived;
in June 2010 she began "secretly" dating 34-year-old Cy Waits who,
along with his identical twin brother Jesse and other partners, opened
and managed several successful Las Vegas nightclubs, including Af-
terhours, Tryst at the Wynn, and XS at Encore. Paris and her family

had apparently known Cy for years and the relationship only recently turned romantic. Cy and Jesse, who is romantically linked with Brody Jenner's ex-girlfriend Jayde Nicole, were both voted "America's Most Eligible Bachelors" by the *Extra* TV show.

While initially Cy had parental approval, no doubt enhanced after he chased off a burglar from Paris's home on August 24, 2010—the man, 31-year-old Nathan Lee Parada, was caught and arrested—things undoubtedly turned dicey a few days later on August 27, when Paris and Cy were pulled over by Las Vegas police outside the Wynn after the smell of marijuana was detected from his vehicle. While a crowd of onlookers grew (and news eventually reached as far as Australia and Europe), Cy was allegedly booked for DUI and possession of illegal substances. A couple of days later, he was fired from his nightclub job. Meanwhile, Paris, in police custody inside the Wynn in Las Vegas, reached inside her purse for a tube of lip balm and a small bundle of cocaine fell out. She was arrested and booked as well but released after only a few hours.

Her excuse was that the incriminating purse (and drugs) belonged to a girlfriend—she had borrowed it (the purse) because it matched her outfit and insisted she had no idea the cocaine was there. However, several weeks earlier, Paris reportedly sent a picture of a suspiciously identical sparkly black Chanel bag over Twitter, writing "Love My New Chanel Purse I got Today."[8]

While she's sticking to her story—and Cy—and claims not to be worried about yet another stint in jail (see chapter 6), she's kept a relatively low profile, vacationing in Maui with him instead of attending the 2010 MTV Video Music Awards, although the producers invited her to be part of it. Paris declined, perhaps wanting to avoid a repeat of her June 2007 appearance, when, after being the target of comedian Sara Silverman, she turned herself in to the LA County jail to begin her sentence. (The producers got Lindsay Lohan, another past and possible future jailbird, instead.)

Only time will tell whether history will repeat itself for Paris; as of this writing, her arraignment has been set in Las Vegas for October 27, 2010, on a possession of cocaine charge. Her alleged hookups have been extensive and controversial, with varying levels of involvement, depending upon who is asked. They almost read like a Hollywood who's who and include (in no particular order) Oscar De La Hoya, Brandon Davis, Criss Angel, Nick Lachey, Leonardo DiCaprio, Robert Evans, Colin Farrell, Edward Furlong, Vincent Gallo, Jamie Kennedy, Josh Henderson, Brody Jenner, Jared Leto, Robert Mills (fifth place in 2003's *Australian Idol*), Mark Philippoussis, Simon Rex, Jake Sumner (son of Sting), Deryck Whibley, Tom Sizemore, and Joe Francis.[9]

Many famous people have supposedly had hundreds if not thousands of romantic liaisons, the late president John F. Kennedy being an obvious example, despite his bad back and other health problems and having to run the country and spend time with his wife and young children. So such exaggerations and wild speculations are nothing new. Today, however, just about any photo, video, or sound track can be concocted and distributed, thanks to computers and digital media and the worldwide accessibility that the Internet provides. So anyone can see "pictures" or download "videos" of Paris indulging in drugs and having relations with various males as well as making out with celebrity lesbian Ingrid Casares, MTV personality Eglantina Zingg, and Playboy Playmate Nicole Lenz.[10] Whether such film clips and photos are authentic is another story.

While Paris has admitted that she sometimes falls in love too fast—and that it can get her into trouble—she finds such exposure a horrible violation of her privacy. "I'm basically being judged and I can't do anything about it," she laments. "I could [file] lawsuits and spend millions of dollars" trying to stop publication of the tsunami of gossip she seems to generate. "Probably 90 percent of the stuff I read about myself is completely fabricated . . . or just so untrue that it's like a joke." So she has learned to block it out, even though it bothers her, her family, and her friends.[11]

Sister Nicky's choice of men has also been somewhat chaotic, tending toward the A-list, although her love life has not been as visible or wide-ranging as that of her sister. In 2003, she dated MTV VJ Brian McFayden and actor Ian Somerhalder of *Lost* fame. The next year, however, she wed family friend and New York businessman Todd Meister, who was 12 years her senior; however, the union was annulled just three months later. Apparently he had difficulty keeping up with her party-hearty lifestyle, as 4 A.M. can look vastly different to a 21-year-old than to someone in their mid-30s. She went on to date *Entourage* actor Kevin Connolly and since 2006 has been romantically linked to actress Ashley Olsen's ex-boyfriend, producer David Katzenberg, son of billionaire DreamWorks Animation CEO Jeffrey Katzenberg. There have been rumors of a wedding, although no official plans or dates have been set.

FROM BOYFRIENDS TO GIRL FIGHTS

While Nicky tends to stick to guys with less volatile—or at least vocally visible—ex-wives or girlfriends, Paris often found herself in the middle of feuds, many of which revolve around men, the notable exception being Nicole Richie. Some of the rivalries have been exaggerated or egged on by the press and fueled by competition over looks or fame. Some of the more well-known grudges include:

Lindsay Lohan

Paris's 2006 feud with actress and rehab frequent flier Lindsay Lohan apparently had its origins over Stavros Niarchos, whom Paris was dating at the time. Paris left for a trip to Australia, and Niarchos was spotted flirting and dancing with Lohan at an LA nightclub. When asked about the supposed affair de Niarchos, Paris retorted, "That was crap. She's never even hung out with Stavros. He thinks she's pathetic."[12]

In apparent retaliation, a widely circulated film clip from the celebrity news Web site TMZ showed Paris giggling wildly while a very drunk oil heir Brandon Davis made scatological remarks about Lohan's anatomy. Lohan was understandably upset, and the media severely criticized Paris, lambasting Davis as a crude and total waste of space. In true spin doctor style, Paris's longtime (and now former) publicist Elliot Mintz tried to smooth over the incident by pointing out that Paris was only laughing at Davis and not saying anything. After trading a few barbs back and forth—including an accusation by Lohan that Paris and Davis hacked into her voice mail and made prank calls—Lindsay and Paris made up in October of that year by going to Las Vegas to gamble and party.

They have been on-and-off again frenemies ever since.

Jessica Simpson

The roots of this rivalry apparently began in 1998, when Paris reportedly dated and was dumped by musician Nick Lachey. He later fell in love with and married singer Jessica Simpson, and Paris has supposedly resented Jessica ever since.

Saturday Night Live comedienne Tina Fey claimed that when Paris guest starred on the show, she specifically requested an opportunity to parody Simpson because she (Simpson) was fat. However, the antagonism seems to mostly exist in the media and on the Internet, with the two facing off over competing lines of hair extensions, shoes, and even music videos and reality shows. Few if any actual confrontations seem to have taken place.

Shanna Moakler

In contrast, Paris and actress Shanna Moakler supposedly duked it out in a nightclub in 2006. They had been friends until Paris was spotted kissing Moakler's estranged husband, Travis Barker. As a result of the altercation, both filed police reports claiming that the other had assaulted her. Paris asserted that Shanna punched her in the jaw after shouting at her, while Moakler maintained that one of Paris's boyfriends shoved her down a set of stairs. Moakler had also allegedly been leaving threatening messages on the heiress's voice mail. Neither woman commented publicly about the nightclub brawl.

Mischa Barton

The year 2006 was a banner one for Paris feuds. Alleged bad blood supposedly started boiling with former O.C. star Mischa Barton, who began dating Cisco Adler, the ex-boyfriend of Paris's good pal Kimberly Stewart. Other reports traced the purported feud to Barton's loyalty to at-the-time-former BFF Nicole Richie. On her end, Barton remarked that Paris "seems to hate everyone around her age who is more successful," rather illogically adding that Paris "steals people's boyfriends." However, Barton also added, "Paris isn't my rival. I met her one or two times and she's making out there's this big rivalry between us and there so isn't."[13]

Paris countered by stating that she had never met Barton. "It seems like she is the one who is trying to stir up a rivalry. I have never said a word about her in my life. But she seems to be spending a lot of time thinking about me."[14] Sounds more like a slow week in the news media than an actual altercation.

Kim Kardashian and Her Sisters

The most recent of the Paris feuds (2007–9)—and again, nonfeud might be a better description—had as its roots a friendship between the reality show stars and celebutantes who bolstered each other's careers by attending various bashes together and hanging out on the Hollywood scene. Various sources claimed that the friendship soured as Kim's fame (and breast size) increased. "Even when I would talk to editors of magazines and other media outlets about featuring Kim, they would comment on how they are moving past Paris in hopes to bring someone fresh to the spotlight, like Kim," Kardashian's ex-rep, Jonathan Jaxson, noted.[15]

Sniped another source: "Now the Kardashians have it all, the reality shows, the magazine covers, the big appearance fees and promotional deals. [Paris] used to command $100,000 for club appearances, but now Kim is the hottest girl. The magazines are bidding around $300,000 for Kourtney's baby-shower and baby pictures. And Khloe's wedding brought in record ratings for E!.

"Paris has realized that standing for excess in a recession doesn't appeal," the source continued. "The Kardashian girls seem more real, and girls identify with them more. She's got to ditch the pink Bentley and concentrate on developing herself."[16]

On her end Paris had no comment, although another unnamed source pointed out that Paris was working hard building up her various product lines and had pretty much settled down. And regarding all of these feuds, real or otherwise, Paris has remarked that they are mostly made up, claiming that's she's actually rather shy and nonconfrontational. "Certain girls just use me to get media attention because a feud with Paris Hilton always gets press."[17] As indeed it seems to do.

I WANT TO BE A HILTON . . . OR
AT LEAST LIVE LIKE ONE

Before the recession slammed the economy, being a Hilton—or at least living like one—was considered almost chic. So in 2005 the Hilton family Christmas was copiously and enthusiastically covered in the press, with "Dr. Christmas" (real name: Bob Pranga), celebrity holiday decorator to the stars, adorning their Bel Air home with two lavishly decorated trees laden with designer baubles and synthetic snow and a life-sized, stuffed Santa surrounded by dolls in winter clothes. Not that Kathy, Rick, and the four kids were going to be around to enjoy it; they planned to spend that yuletide at a Four Seasons (not a Hilton) in Maui, with dinner at Spago and lunch at Ferraro's. Then it was off to Vegas for the New Year, with Paris and Nicky hosting respective parties at the Venetian and Caesar's Palace. "Luckily the two venues aren't too far apart, so we'll be able to go to both," observed Kathy.[18]

Although in 2005 Paris didn't get her asked-for Bentley—she did purchase a customized pink one for herself a few years later—and $100,000 diamond earrings, Kathy was plenty generous, buying the girls personalized Carolina Herrera winter shrugs (pink for Paris and blue for Nicky), and designer blouses, dresses, and trousers, along with Jimmy Choo shoes. But the "big" present turned out to be Monica Rich Kosann sterling silver picture frames and charm bracelets, along with a photo shoot with the selfsame designer, who was also a celebrity photographer. "I always have to make sure that the girls get exactly the same thing because, whenever they don't, they end up fighting," Kathy said. Some things never change, no matter how old one gets. The boys, Barron, then 16, and Conrad, 11, "were easy to buy for . . . they'll get an Xbox and video games."[19]

The many Hilton pets received presents as well, most notably sterling silver nametags by designer Kosann. Supposed to be included in the bounty was Baby Luv, an exotic kinkajou monkey that more resembled a fuzzy raccoon with a Chihuahua face, acquired by Paris on a recent trip to Las Vegas. Unfortunately it turned out to be illegal to own a monkey in LA, and a few weeks before Christmas authorities from the California Department for Fish and Game stopped by to take Baby Luv away as Paris sobbed hysterically. "Paris adores animals but she's too impulsive and often buys exotic pets without understanding how to care for them or whether they can legally be kept as pets," a Hilton insider was quoted as saying. The same thing happened with a baby kangaroo she had shipped home while filming in Queensland, Australia. "She was forced to send it back when she discovered they grow up to be very violent," the source added. Paris had "had no idea she was breaking the law" when she purchased the animals, a pattern that was to repeat itself with even more serious consequences a few months down the road.[20]

Nevertheless life chez Hilton was appealing enough that producers from NBC-TV thought it might make a good reality show, a sort of companion piece to *The Simple Life* (in fact it was originally titled to *The Good Life*). So, also in 2005, Kathy agreed to host *I Want to Be a Hilton*, a reality competition with 14 wannabes from around the United States eager to learn the ways of the upper crust. Husband Rick was a producer.

Sort of a 21st-century take on *The Beverly Hillbillies*, the show put up contestants in a fancy New York hotel; whether or not it was Hilton-owned was never fully disclosed. Also, like on the reality shows *The Apprentice* and *Survivor*, aspirants were divided into two competing teams: "Park" and "Madison." The payoff for winning this boot camp for etiquette and manners included a $200,000 trust fund along with a New York apartment, a wardrobe, and the chance to live like high society for one year.

Contenders came from all over the United States and all walks of life and included a clerk from the Bureau of Motor Vehicles, a Las Vegas dancer, a golf caddy, a ranch hand, and a plumber. Two even resided in trailer parks. In each episode, they struggled to excel at tasks ranging from dog grooming to putting on a fashion show to organizing a charity event and were exposed to the finer aspects of art, culture, beauty, and fashion. A tastefully dressed and coiffed Kathy guided them through the challenges with surprise visits and critiques from Paris, Nicky, and other family members, friends, and arbiters of good taste such as Ted Allen, culinary expert from the *Queer Eye for the Straight Guy* TV show; Billy Bush from *Access Hollywood*; and His Royal Highness, Prince Dimitri of Yugoslavia (who?). At the end of each episode, Kathy met with the losing team and, in a nod to Donald Trump's infamous "You're fired!" eliminated one contestant with the catch phrase, "Sorry, you're not on the list," with a gracious and apologetic smile.

Although *I Want to Be a Hilton* had its share of detractors and critics and was itself excluded from NBC's "list" for the next season, it was a kinder, gentler reality show, as Kathy herself pointed out, a kind of *My Fair Lady* meets *The Apprentice*. And some reviewers praised her dignified and even-handed treatment of contestants. "I don't think we needed to humiliate people or say the f-word to have a good show," she remarked.[21]

The winner, hunky-looking and good natured Jaret Elwood, was a 26-year-old telephone salesman and kindergarten teacher from Rendon, Texas, who liked to refer to himself as a sophisticated redneck. A graduate of Texas Tech College, at one time he ranked number one in the state in the 800-meter race. His hobbies included (not surprisingly) running track, spending time with his own family, including his twin sister, fishing, and other sports. He did hang around with the Hiltons—Kathy making good on her insinuation that the winner would be considered part of her family—showing up at gallery openings, charitable events, and even at Rick's birthday party in the late summer and fall of 2005. However this only lasted a few weeks, as he supposedly went back to Texas and never showed up on the celebrity radar again.

Kathy had one last word to add about her show. "Reputation is something you can't buy. It takes 20 or 30 years to make your reputation and ten minutes to blow it."[22] Because of the Salomon sex tape, she might have hoped that Paris's 15 minutes of infamy had only dented her daughter's social standing, but an even greater storm lay ahead.

JAIL TIME—NOT HOT!

Paris, Nicky, and Nicole Richie have all had run-ins with the law, although in comparison to Paris, her former BFF and little sister came off relatively unscathed. In December 2006, while still filming *The Simple Life*, Nicole was arrested in the wee hours of the morning after she drove her black Mercedes-Benz SUV the wrong way on a freeway in Burbank. Pregnant with her first baby, she was en route from the home of the child's father and her significant other, Joel Madden. She reportedly told authorities that she had smoked marijuana and taken the prescription painkiller Vicodin. This was her second DUI conviction; her first occurred in June 2003, the same year she checked into rehab after being arrested for heroin possession and driving with a revoked license.

In July 2006, Nicole was sentenced to four days in jail, fined $2,048, and required to sign up for a driving rehab course. She reported to the Century Regional Detention Facility in Lynwood on August 24 but served a mere 82 minutes there due to overcrowded conditions. However, there was no escaping the 18-month anti-drinking driver education program, which consisted of 52 hours of group counseling, biweekly face-to-face interviews, and 12 hours of alcohol education as well as attendance at 12-step meetings.

However, unlike her former BFF, who appeared not to care or simply ignored what was developing around her, Nicole appeared humble and contrite, cooperating with authorities and readily admitting her fault in the matter. Along with swearing off alcohol, drugs, and cigarettes—a vow she seems to have kept so far—she has admitted, "Every mistake I make, there's consequences. I don't take anything lightly."[23]

In contrast, Paris's sister Nicky actually took the law into her own hands. In February 2009 she was accosted by a homeless man outside of an International House of Pancakes (IHOP) in West Hollywood, shortly after just finishing a 5 A.M. breakfast. The man, Michael Broadhurst, knocked her over, later claiming he thought she was his girlfriend. Nicky promptly got back up and made a citizen's arrest. By coincidence, or perhaps due to Hilton luck, a deputy sheriff happened to be at the IHOP on a coffee break, saw the commotion, and immediately called for backup. The homeless fellow was charged with a misdemeanor battery known as an unwanted touching, and Nicky emerged as somewhat of a heroine, a celebutante with backbone.

Paris would have preferred not to deal with the judicial system at all, or at least not on the same level as the rest of humanity. "[Cops] just pull me over to hit on me," she has said. "They're like, 'What's your phone number?' 'Want to go to dinner?'" adding, "I think I get in more trouble because of who I am."[24]

True or not, the facts remain the same. At approximately 12:30 A.M. on Thursday, September 7, 2006, Paris was pulled over by officers of the Los Angeles Police Department (LAPD) for reckless operation of her Mercedes. "She exhibited the symptoms of intoxication," stated Officer Robert Andreno. "The vehicle was driving erratically and they conducted a field sobriety test at the scene and the officers determined she was driving under the influence."[25] Paris's blood alcohol level was .08, the minimum level for a DUI arrest in the state of California.

Kimberly Stewart, daughter of singer Rod, was with Paris at the time; they were coming home from a charity benefit for brain cancer patients, where Paris claimed to have only had a single margarita. Hosted by guitarist Dave Navarro, formerly of Jane's Addiction and the Red Hot Chili Peppers, the gala was held at the West Hollywood hotspot Dragon Fly and included a concert by Suicide Girls. Paris had also spent the day shooting a music video for her recently released debut album, *Paris*. The DUI was "probably the result of an empty stomach and working all day and being fatigued," explained Elliot Mintz, her publicist at the time.[26] Paris herself claimed to have been up for 24 hours and to have had nothing to eat and no rest for the entire day.

Initially the officers didn't even know exactly who they had pulled over. However, after determining that her blood alcohol was at the level at which an adult driver is in violation of the law and after she failed the sobriety test, they arrested her and took her to the LAPD Hollywood division, where she was booked, only be released on her own recognizance about an hour later. In addition to the mass of paparazzi who apparently must have been listening to the police scanner, sister Nicky, Nicky's boyfriend at the time, *Entourage* star Kevin Connolly, and publicist Mintz were there to greet her after she was released.

Although Paris expressed regret over the escapade, she downplayed the reckless driving part. "Everything I do is blown out of proportion and it really hurts my feelings. So maybe I was speeding a little bit and I got pulled over. . . . I was just really hungry and wanted an In-And-Out Burger."[27]

It was to be an expensive sandwich, even by Hilton standards. If convicted, she could receive a six-month jail sentence and be ordered to pay a $1,000 fine. As a first-time offender, her license was suspended for six months from November 2006 until March 2007, with a letter stating same sent to her Beverly Hills business office. In January 2007 she pleaded no contest to a reckless driving charge, with a penalty of 36 months probation and fines of about $1,500. She was also required to enroll in an alcohol education program by February 12 of that year. Publicist Mintz considered the case closed: "She told me that she was happy the matter is over," he said.[28]

And it would have been, had Paris honored the terms of her sentence. But she couldn't stay off of the roads. In December 2006, she was nabbed in Hollywood for making an illegal turn and warned that her license was invalid. About a month later, on January 15, she was pulled over by California Highway Patrol (CHP) officers who informed her once again that she was driving on a suspended license. According to some accounts, she was stopped because her vehicle lacked front and back license plates. (As if that crucial omission would prevent the police from noticing her or her car—what was she thinking?) She signed a document acknowledging that she was not supposed to drive, putting her copy of the papers in her glove compartment; the originals went on file in the courts.

Then at 11 P.M. on February 27, Paris was pulled over yet again, this time by Los Angeles County sheriff's deputies, for speeding 70 mph in a 35 mph zone with her headlights off. This time, both Paris and her 2007 Bentley convertible were incarcerated—Paris was cited and arrested for driving on a suspended license and released a short time later and her vehicle impounded. Her excuse, according to Mintz, was that she'd just left a brightly lit parking lot and forgot to turn her headlights on. No explanation was offered as to why she'd failed to enroll in the alcohol education course.

But as minor as these violations seemed to be, they had a cumulative effect, giving the LA city attorneys enough evidence to build their case to revoke her probation and possibly send her to jail. The city prosecutor asked the judge to sentence her to 45 days, and in April of that year, Paris was charged with violating her probation and ordered to appear before the court.

May 4, 2007, is a date that Paris will likely never forget. She showed up 10 minutes late at the Los Angeles Metropolitan Courthouse—hardly an auspicious beginning—somberly clad in black pants, a white blouse, and a grey jacket with Christian Louboutin heels and a Chanel bag, with parents Rick and Kathy in tow. As if at a red carpet event, dozens of photographers and reporters lined the rear entrance; only yellow police tape substituted for velvet ropes.

Inside, the press bench was jam-packed and nine bailiffs made sure there was order in the court, far more than even for a high-profile murder case. "We go upstairs and everyone's out of their offices on every floor, staring at us like we were monkeys," recalled Kathy. "They all wanted to get a look at Paris."[29] Paris appeared composed as she checked her makeup before being called to testify, although she'd allegedly confided to a friend that she didn't know what she was going to do if she even had to spend even a single day in jail.

Kathy later admitted to *UK Daily Mail* reporter Rebecca Hardy that Paris didn't really believe she was going to be incarcerated, although Kathy's media contacts had privately warned them to expect the worst. "I told Paris, 'You're going to jail,'" Kathy said. Although "I . . . thought it would be a week, ten days, tops."[30]

During the two-hour hearing, Paris took the witness stand and stated that her publicist Elliot Mintz had repeatedly informed her that her license had only been suspended for 30 days and that she could still drive for work-related matters. Had she known otherwise, "I never would've been driving," she testified. "I follow the law. I'm followed by cameras every single day."[31] Mintz himself also took the stand and backed up her statements. In their case against her, the prosecutors called the officers who had pulled her over on the three separate occasions, bringing up the fact that she'd acknowledged the suspension of her license in writing and failed to sign up for her court-ordered alcohol education class. When asked about the first, Paris posed the rather weak defense that she had not read what she was signing. "I was just signing it because the officer told me to," she said, unintentionally inciting jokes and banter between judge and the attorneys, much to the dismay of Kathy and Rick.[32]

Before the sentence was delivered, Paris was asked to make one last statement before the court. Seeming truly contrite and upset, she said, "I respect the law. . . . I want you to know I'm very sorry and will pay complete attention to everything from now on."[33]

Alas, it was too little, too late. After hearing the arguments from both sides, the presiding judge of the Superior Court, Michael Sauer, figuratively threw the book at Paris, calling Mintz's testimony worthless and pointing to what he referred to as the "smoking gun"—the written warning verifying suspension of her license that she'd signed after being pulled over by the CHP.

"I can't believe that [her] attorney did not tell her that the suspension had been upheld," he said. "She wanted to disregard everything that was said and continue to drive no matter what."[34] He then sentenced her to 45 days at the Century Regional Detention Facility, an all-female prison in Lynwood, California.

This was no cushy "country club" minimum security institution. "Forty-five days [there] is really rough. That's an awful, hellish place," observed criminal defense attorney Dana Cole. "Conditions are miserable, people take showers under cold dripping water, the food is completely inedible."[35] Along with the requisite orange jumpsuit and canvas slip-on shoes, Paris was to be confined to an 8-by-12-foot cell, her jewel-encrusted cell phone confiscated—all inmates waited in line for use of a bank of pay phones in the common area—with no makeup and certainly no hair extensions.

Both Paris and her parents look stunned as the sentence was pronounced, and then Paris started sobbing. Kathy gasped and became angry, shouting at the prosecutors, "You're pathetic," and sarcastically asking the judge, "Can I have your autograph?" Several months after Paris's release, when her daughter was home safe and sound, Kathy referred to Sauer as sadistic and publicity-hungry, adding that she wanted to humiliate him by asking for his autograph, now that he had gotten his 15 minutes of fame for putting her daughter in jail.

"I'm shocked and disappointed at the sentence by the judge," Paris's attorney, Howard Weitzman, told the news media outside. "To sentence Paris Hilton to jail is uncalled for, inappropriate and ludicrous. She was singled out for who she is. She's been selectively targeted. Paris was honest in her testimony. Shame on the system." He added that he'd represented many second- and third-time DWI offenders who'd never received jail time.

The Hiltons planned to appeal the sentence. In fact, the next day, May 5, Paris admirer and self-proclaimed friend Joshua Morales organized an online petition on Paris's MySpace page asking Governor Arnold Schwarzenegger for a pardon. "Please allow her to her return to her career and life," the petition stated. "Everyone makes mistakes. She didn't hurt or kill anyone, and she has learned her lesson. She is sincere, apologetic, and full of regret for her actions as she explained tearfully to the Judge handling her case in court yesterday. She is distraught and understandably afraid."[36]

But almost as quickly and in response, opponents created a counterpetition to uphold the sentence, which said in part, "For as long as she has been in the public spotlight, Paris Hilton has knowingly and willingly broken the law, and her actions have gotten more and more brazen over the last few years. . . . She feels the law doesn't apply to her as she has repeatedly flaunted [it] in full view of witnesses, often paparazzi and camera crews."[37]

Both petitions attracted thousands of signatures, and Paris switched lawyers. She also fired and then rehired publicist Mintz, resolving, in his words, an apparent "misunderstanding she received from me regarding the terms of her probation."[38]

Many thought, including Paris and her family, that she would get off with a slap on the wrist or at most a day or two in the Big House, a fine, and maybe some community service or confinement to quarters with an ankle bracelet. But as with Marie Antoinette before her, it was not a question of the punishment fitting the crime, which was actually for driving with a suspended license rather than a DUI. Luckily it was the 21st century and guillotines were outlawed, at least in North America.

NOTES

1. "Paris Is Not Promiscuous!" RadarOnline, published Jan. 6, 2009, by www.theinsider.com/news/1505653_Paris_is_not_promiscuous.

2. "Randy Spelling: I Took Paris's Virginity," WENN.com (March 27, 2007), www.hollywood.com/news/Randy_Spelling_I_Took_Paris_Virginity/3673792.

3. Ibid.

4. Chas Newkey-Burden, *Paris Hilton: Life on the Edge* (London: John Blake, 2007), 75.

5. Ibid, 65.

6. "Paris Hilton's Sexless Year," *Female First* (Nov. 11, 2006), www.femalefirst.co.uk/celebrity/Paris+Hilton-10606.html.

7. Joanna Sloame, "Paris Hilton Bares Scary Skinny Bikini Bod While Ex Doug Reinhardt Steps out with Paris Look-Alike," *New York Daily News* (April 26, 2010), www.nydailynews.com/gossip/2010/04/26/2010-04-26_paris_hilton_bares_painfully_thin_bikini_bod_post breakup_with_doug_reinhrein.html#ixzz0mDfn1fe0.

8. Mark Gray, "Did Paris Hilton Post Picture of Cocaine Purse Before Arrest?" People.com (Sept 2, 2010), http://www.people.com/people/article/0,,20418350,00.html.

9. "Paris Hilton," Notable Names Database (Beta version), www.nndb.com/people/479/000023410, accessed May 29, 2010.

10. Ibid.

11. *Paris, Not France*, directed by Adria Petty, documentary (New York: MTV, 2008), unpublished transcript.

12. "Paris Passes on Dallas Movie . . . Sex for a Year . . . and Tony Blair Recognition" (Aug. 4, 2006), www.thehollywoodgossip.com/categories/paris-hilton/page/39.

13. "Take That! Top Celebrity Showdowns," *New York Daily News* (n.d.), www.nydailynews.com/gossip/toplists/take_that_top_celebrity_showdowns/take_that_top_celebrity_showdowns.html#ixzz0YT MlokAb.

14. Bryan Alexander and Stephen M. Silverman, "Mischa, Paris Take off the Gloves," People.com (Feb. 22, 2006), www.people.com/people/article/0,,1161912,00.html.

15. "Kim Kardashian and Paris Hilton: No Longer BFF," The Hollywood Gossip (April 10, 2007), www.thehollywoodgossip.com/2007/04/kim-karadshian-and-paris-hilton-no-longer-bff.

16. "Paris Hilton Sparks Feud with Kim Kardashian and Her Sisters," Live Journal (Nov. 15, 2009), community.livejournal.com/ohnotheydidnt/41139480.html.

17. "Paris Hilton: I Don't Have Ongoing Feuds—They're Made Up," Fametastic (July 25, 2006), fametastic.co.uk/archive/20060725/1942/paris-hilton-i-dont-have-ongoing-feuds-theyre-made-up.

18. Lina Das, "Bling in the New: What Do You Get a Hilton for Christmas?" *Daily Mail* (London) (Dec. 24, 2005): 6.

19. Ibid.

20. "Paris Hilton's Monkey Confiscated," *Female First* (n.d.), www.femalefirst.co.uk/celebrity/Paris+Hilton-7392.html.

21. Mike Hughes, "Kathy's Turn! Hiltons' Mother Gets Her Own Shot at Stardom with Reality Show," Gannett News Service (June 3, 2005), electronic database access [Proquest].

22. Rebecca Hardy, "Passport to Paris," *Daily Mail* (London) (Nov. 5, 2005): 20.

23. Laura Brown, "Partners in Crime," *Harper's Bazaar* 3547 (June 2007): 134.

24. Ibid.

25. Gil Kaufman, "Paris Hilton Arrested for Suspicion of Drunk Driving," MTV news (Sept. 8, 2006), www.mtv.com/news/articles/1540341/20060907/hilton_paris.jhtml.

26. Ibid.

27. Ibid.

28. "Paris Hilton Pleads No Contest to DUI Charge," Associated Press (Jan. 22, 2007), www.msnbc.msn.com/id/16757099.

29. Rebecca Hardy, "So, Mrs. Hilton, Are You Ashamed of Your Daughter?" *Daily Mail* (London) (May 23, 2008): 15.

30. Ibid.

31. Ken Lee, "Paris Hilton Gets 45 Days in Jail," People.com (May 4, 2007), www.people.com/people/article/0,,20037947,00.html.

32. Newkey-Burden, *Paris Hilton*, 230.

33. Lee, "Paris Hilton Gets 45 Days."

34. "Paris Hilton Sentenced to 45 Days in Jail for Probation Violation," Fox News (May 4, 2007), www.foxnews.com/story/0,2933,269890,00.html.

35. "For Paris Hilton, Jail Will Be an 'Awful, Hellish Place,'" ABC News.com/GMA (May 5, 2007), http://abcnews.go.com/GMA/story?id=3143374&page=1.

36. "'Free Paris Hilton!' Petition Begs," CBS News.com (May 8, 2007), www.cbsnews.com/stories/2007/05/08/entertainment/main2773021.shtml.

37. Counter-petition, www.ipetitions.com/petition/jailparishilton.

38. "'Free Paris Hilton!' Petition Begs."

Chapter 6

TURNAROUND TIME

The Century Regional Detention Facility (CRDF), where Paris was to be incarcerated, houses nearly 2,200 women and was Mars compared to Venus, Paris's childhood residence at the Waldorf-Astoria. Inmates are only permitted to leave their cells for an hour a day to make phone calls, take a shower, watch TV, or exercise. The bland menu consists of "mystery meat" with overcooked, unseasoned vegetables and starches. Cells have bunks with lumpy mattresses, open toilets and sinks, and six-inch windows. A nearby freeway and train tracks add to the post-apocalyptic ambiance.

It could have been worse. Paris could have been sent to the Twin Towers County Jail, home of California's most hardened criminals, including Charles Manson, murderer of actress Sharon Tate. But the point—at first, anyway—was to teach her a lesson rather than harm her or make her the object of hostile (or amorous) prisoner or gang attention. "Her biggest problem is going to be boredom," defense attorney Sean Tabibian told the media. "How many conversations can you have with yourself?" (Many of his clients are CRDF alumni.) For her safety, Paris would also be segregated from the general population, living in a one- or two-person cell, and was supposed be given a "panic button," a device providing a 24-hour link to prison guards in case she encountered trouble.

And the inmates were looking forward to meeting their famous resident, although other celebrities had made brief appearances at CRDF, including Lindsay Lohan (84 minutes), Daryl Hannah, and *Lost* star Michelle Rodriguez (a few hours) as well as Paris's own BFF, Nicole Richie (82 minutes). "She'll be fine as long as she doesn't come in saying 'I'm Paris Hilton' with an attitude," said former prisoner and convicted drunk driver Jasmine Garrison.[1] Not only would Paris's presence help break the monotony, but with part of the Hilton fortune in her canteen account, she'd have plenty of friends.

Understandably, Paris felt quite different. The day after sentencing, she went shopping with her mother in Beverly Hills and broke down sobbing during lunch at Prego. "I told the truth yesterday," she confided to the press. "The sentence is both cruel and unwanted and I don't deserve this."[2] Be that as it may, how she would handle the experience would have a major impact on her life. It could set the stage for a comeback a la Martha Stewart or Robert Downey Jr. or could be the beginning of a downward spiral into obscurity—or worse.

FROM 90210 TO PRISONER #9818783

Initially Judge Sauer ordered Paris to begin her sentence immediately, but her lawyers argued for a stay of execution, stating that she had personal matters to attend to; specifically, a scheduled appearance at the MTV Awards in LA on June 3. So she was to report at the prison on or before Tuesday, June 5. With good behavior and to help eliminate overcrowding, police officials speculated, her 45-day sentence would be almost halved to 23 days. When the reduced sentence was officially confirmed, Paris dropped her appeal, no doubt wanting to avoid further courtroom drama.

However, Sauer refused to bend on concessions often given to similar or first-time offenders—alternative sentencing such as work release or furlough; incarceration in a minimum security jail or halfway house; or electronic monitoring. Nor could Paris pay to serve time in a jail of her choice, as some celebrities or high-profile individuals had been allowed to do in the past.

So Paris apparently turned her attentions to a higher power in hopes of helping her cause. Along with being seen and photographed carrying a Bible and a spiritual book, *The Power of Now,* she was spotted shopping at the Bodhi Tree, a Buddhist store in Hollywood, and wore lots of white, resulting in speculation that she was trying to appear pure. She minimized the partying and toned down her trademark skimpy outfits and glitz and seemed calm and in control.

Sources close to her saw a different side, however. Paris "has been having such a tough time with it all despite her going out with friends and going shopping," confided one, adding that along with not eating, she'd been breaking down and crying a lot. "Her parents and friends are beyond worried about her," despite her attempts to stay normal. Other, however, were not as supportive. "As for her friends, that's been another spot of stress for Paris. She really can't take how most people around her have scattered and distanced themselves."[3]

But on her last night of freedom, Paris had a small but significant triumph at the MTV Awards. Clad in an elegant black dress and glittering jewels, with her famous blonde locks tumbling over a bare right shoulder, she exuded style and class as she settled into a seat near the stage, a prime target for acerbic comedienne Sarah Silverman. But Paris took Silverman's off-color jokes on exposed body parts and jail time in stride and stayed for almost the entire show. Then she left—not for some glamorous after-party, as was expected, but to report to jail. So while most paparazzi were chasing other stars, Paris turned in her possessions and was medically screened and strip-searched, the latter being the most humiliating experience of her life, she later confided to radio personality Larry King. She was also photographed, only this time by prison officials, with nary a reporter in sight. They issued her standard prison garb, orange two-piece cotton/polyester-blend uniforms produced by Los Angeles County inmates in sewing classes. Paris was then handcuffed and led to her private cell in a section of the prison reserved for high-profile inmates.

"I am ready to face the consequences of violating probation," she said in a media statement through her lawyer Richard Hutton. "During the past few weeks, I have had a lot of time to think and have come to realize I made some mistakes.

"This is an important point in my life and I need to take responsibility for my actions," she continued through the statement. "In the future, I plan on taking more of an active role in the decisions I make. . . . Although I am scared, I am ready to begin my jail sentence." Brave words, but the reality was a lot harder than the hotel heiress who had been raised in the midst of luxury could imagine.

BE THE COUNTY'S GUEST

Paris soon discovered that jail was anything but a *Simple Life* romp where she could try things out and walk away should they become too disgusting or difficult. There were no cameras or makeup artists or star trailers or BFFs to make things easier or more fun. And while she had always been an adventuresome soul, game for everything from jetting to Japan for a day of shopping and product promotion to changing diapers in a day-care center, she quickly found the confinement and uncomfortable conditions of jail intolerable. By day two she complained that her cell was too cold, she had no pillow, the food was awful, and the other prisoners too noisy. Some were friendly—chants of "Paris! Paris!" could be heard; one prisoner gifted her with an origami butterfly and another provided her with a notepad to be used as a diary or for drawing for the 23 hours or so she was alone in her cell.

But others, not so much, according to her mother Kathy. "There were rumors that the inmates were going to do this or that to her," she said. "People were even throwing excrement at the window of her cell."[4] While Paris herself never copped to that occurring, she did tell radio host Larry King that, while the inmates seemed friendly enough, she sometimes had nightmares about someone breaking into her cell and doing harm to her.

And Paris was making herself physically ill with stress, loneliness, and fear. "She cries all day," stated a prison source. "She looks unwashed, she has no makeup and her hair is tangled. She cried audibly through the first two nights."[5] While her lawyer, Richard Hutton, one of two permitted weekday visitors (the other was a psychiatrist, Dr. Charles Sophy), told reporters that she was bearing up well, by day five, Thursday, she was released due to an unspecified medical condition, although speculation ran from everything from refusal to eat the food to claustrophobia to a mysterious rash; or perhaps a combination of all these.

Later it came to light, in a *People* magazine article published after she'd completed her sentence, that Paris had attention deficit disorder and was being treated for the condition with counseling and medication (Adderall) before she went to jail, which, unbeknownst to prison officials, she stopped taking once behind bars. A central nervous system stimulant prescribed for attention deficit/hyperactivity disorder (ADHD), Adderall affects chemicals in the brain and nerves contributing to impulse control, and Paris had been taking it for years. During her 74 hours in county lockup, "She practically had a nervous breakdown," stated a family friend.[6]

And it appeared that the (police) force was with her, at least in the form of Los Angeles County Sheriff Lee Baca, who signed her release order and reassigned her to home detention. The county jail was not equipped to treat the "various psychological and psychiatric issues" that Paris appeared to be suffering from.[7] It also helped that Baca was somewhat sympathetic to her cause: "My message to those who don't like celebrities is that punishing celebrities more than the average American is not justice," adding that "the special treatment, in a sense, appears to be because of her celebrity status. . . . She got more time in jail."[8]

After her release, she was fitted with an ankle bracelet and her original 45-day sentence reinstated—since she'd enjoy the confines of her Hollywood Hills home instead of a 12-by-8-foot cell—with credit for five days served. Terms of house arrest included a radius limited to 75–100 feet from her home; she could not leave the house under any circumstance, including work; and all doctor's appointments had to be cleared beforehand through the proper channels.

"I want to thank the Los Angeles County Sheriff's Department and staff of the Century Regional Detention Center for treating me fairly and professionally," Paris said in a prepared statement via her attorney Hutton. "I have learned a great deal from this ordeal and hope that others have learned from my mistakes."

The reprieve was short-lived, however. Within hours of her release, Judge Sauer demanded that she return to court the next day, June 8. In his original sentencing, he had specifically stated that Paris was not to serve time at home under electronic monitoring. Even Sheriff Baca took flak for potential conflict of interest; the *New York Post* pointed out that celebrities such as Jack Nicholson, Catherine Zeta-Jones, Dustin Hoffman, Barbra Streisand, Sylvester Stallone, and most notably, Paris's paternal grandfather William Barron Hilton, had donated to his election campaign. Baca had also golfed with Michael Douglas and issued a concealed weapon permit to Ben Affleck, and his department was allegedly involved with cover-up of Mel Gibson's anti-Semitic tirade in 2006. The reassignment also sparked outrage across the nation; the LA Board of Supervisors alone received more than 500 angry calls, e-mails, and faxes, and least two supervisors demanded an investigation.[9]

So it was to a circus-like atmosphere that a visibly shaken and tear-streaked Paris came back to the scene of her original condemnation. At her home, before being handcuffed and pushed head-down into the back of a sheriff's car, she embraced her family. Paris had no idea they were coming to get her: "Ten minutes before the police arrived I'm yanked out of bed," she recalled. "[They were] telling me that they're going to handcuff me and then bring me back to the—to the courthouse. I was in complete shock. It was unbelievable. I was terrified."[10]

As Paris was driven off, a deeply distraught Kathy told reporters, "It is what it is and it's in God's hands now. . . . It's out of our hands. There's nothing we can do." As the gates of the driveway opened, Paris's fans rushed the cruiser, screaming while officers tried to restore order by shouting through bullhorns.

Remarked Paris: "It was . . . really scary just to have so many people . . . on the news telling people what street I live on. It's kind of dangerous." Plus, she added, showing true Hilton hospitality even under the direst circumstances, "I feel really bad for my neighbors."[11]

The Paris who entered the courtroom the second time was a far cry from the self-assured, dressed-to-the-nines young woman of the initial trial. Clad in a rumpled gray sweater and slacks, her hair pulled up in a messy ponytail, all remains of makeup wept away, she cried and trembled throughout the hearing. She also appeared to be praying, mouthing, "I love you," to both her parents, who had followed her to the courthouse and were seated behind her. There was no doubt that Paris was truly suffering both physically and mentally and that she was remorseful and had been deeply humbled.

Paris Hilton arrives at her parents' house minutes after being released from jail in Los Angeles, CA, on June 26, 2007. (AP Photo/Dan Steinberg)

However, Judge Sauer remained unconvinced. After hearing arguments from both the LA city attorney and her lawyers, he ruled that the medical records submitted by the sheriff's department provided inadequate reason for her release and declined to be briefed by Paris's attorney in private chambers as to the nature of her condition. Sauer had "seen no evidence, no documents to support the contention that there was a medical condition," court spokesperson Alan Parachini explained later.[12]

As Sauer ordered Paris back to jail to serve the remainder of her original 45-day sentence—which the state's good behavior law automatically reduced to 23 days, less the 5 days served—Paris lost control. "It's not right!" she yelled as deputies approached her. She called to her parents as she was escorted out, her screams and cries echoing in the inside hallway.

As the courtroom emptied, Kathy wept while Rick held her and comforted her. "She went to kiss me goodbye," Kathy later recalled bitterly. "The guards said, 'No' and just took her. . . . Four people were grabbing at her and she was in chains. It wasn't as if she was going to get away."[13] At a slender 115 pounds, Paris was hardly a bulky, hopped-up, tat-handed gangbanger and was no threat to anyone, except perhaps herself.

That afternoon Sheriff Baca admitted defeat: "We've been overruled by the judge, I accept that, and we'll keep her in county jail." He also denied giving her preferential treatment, saying that her three-day incarceration was more than what most low-level offenders serve. "Let's not make a judicial football of this woman," adding that they were going to keep an eye on her to make sure she was safe and as comfortable as possible under the circumstances.[14]

Even legal experts were shocked at what seemed to be excessive punishment due to her celebrity. First-time offenders more typically receive the minimum 10-day sentence "and serve considerably less than that," observed Ronald Jackson, head of the California DUI Lawyers Association. In LA County, most convicts serve no more than 10 percent of their sentences due to budget shortfalls, according to a *Los Angeles Times* report. And the judicial bouncing of Paris to jail and back was, according to Professor Laurie Levenson of LA's Loyola Law School "insane . . . off the charts."[15]

PARIS BURNING TO PARIS LEARNING

But when it came down to it, Paris had to face the situation on her own, and it was up to her to decide how to handle it. Initially, concern about her condition resulted in her being assigned to the medical wing of the Twin Towers Correctional Facility, where she underwent physical and psychological tests. The results were kept under wraps, but shortly after the tests were finished, Paris announced she was no longer appealing the judge's decision. "After meeting with the doctors, I intend to serve my time as ordered by the judge," she said in a statement to the press, adding:

> This is by far the hardest thing I have ever done. During the past several days, I have had a lot of time to reflect and have already learned a bitter but important lesson from this experience.

As I have said before, I hope others will learn from my mistakes. I have also had time to read the mail from my fans. I very much appreciate all of their good wishes and hope they will keep their letters coming.

I must also say that I was shocked to see all of the attention devoted to the amount of time I would spend in jail for what I had done by the media, public and city officials. I would hope going forward that the public and the media will focus on more important things, like the men and women serving our country in Iraq, Afghanistan and other places around the world.

As Paris was finding out, sometimes you simply have to "woman" up and face unpleasant things; and being rich, blonde, famous, and beautiful is no get-out-of-jail-free card; in this instance, it probably worked against her. "I just said to her, 'Honey, we're a strong family. We love you. There's a reason for this,'" Kathy recalled in an interview several months after Paris's release. "Take this as an opportunity to slow down and reflect. You've got to serve your time—there's nothing we can do. So do it with dignity, like a lady."[16]

Paris has always been willing to share her experiences, and jail was no exception. On June 11, while still at the Twin Towers—she was moved to CRDF on the 13th and stayed there until her release 13 days later—she was interviewed via phone by newscaster Barbara Walters. Kathy was also on the line, and Paris called collect, as is prison procedure. While Paris denied being hysterical during her first few days, she admitted to not eating or sleeping and feeling as if she were in a cage—all perfectly normal reactions. She was also hesitant about taking a shower, since anyone could walk in at any time. However, she continued, since she'd accepted her terms of incarceration, she told Walters that she was now a different person:

I used to act dumb. It was an act. I am 26 years old, and that act is no longer cute. It is not who I am, nor do I want to be that person for the young girls who looked up to me. I know now that I can make a difference, that I have the power to do that. I have been thinking that I want to do different things when I am out of here. I have become much more spiritual. God has given me this new chance.[17]

After that, she appeared to be a model prisoner, staying in her cell, writing in her journal, and reading books sent to her by people such as former convict, celebrity minister, and author Marty Angelo, whose "new beginning" she referenced in her first post-incarceration interview with Larry King. Until this time, she'd rarely been alone, and it actually gave her time to think. "I feel like God does make everything happen for a reason," she later told King. "And it gave me a time-out in life just to really find out what is important and what I want to do, figure out who I am. And even though it was really hard, I took that time just to get to know myself."[18] Little was heard from her until her release at 12:15 A.M. PST on Tuesday, June 26. In total she'd served 22 days of her 23-day sentence, counting her day-long home confinement, proportionately far more "hard time" than most inmates, even those with the least socioeconomic advantages.

Her family greeted her with open arms. Paris "looked like she was 12 years old," recalled Kathy. "She had her hair in braids and no make-up. [She] wasn't sure if people were going to be nice or screaming and throwing things."[19] No matter what the reaction, Paris was determined to leave that prison with her head held high, and she recounted in several interviews that seeing her family and experiencing freedom again made this one of the happiest days of her life.

But as she emerged, "everyone was cheering and screaming support," continued Kathy. "She ran to the car and hugged us . . . People on the freeway were beeping. It was like the craziest thing."[20]

However, as is typical of her, she wasted no time in granting the King interview the day after her release—once she got her hair re-streaked and makeup done, of course. Even the paps were supportive as her limo pulled up to CNN's Los Angeles studios, shouting, "Paris, we love you!" and asking what she'd learned in jail. However, the aftereffects of her jail trauma lasted for several weeks: according to Kathy, Paris cried uncontrollably the first few days after her release and stayed up until all hours of the night reading letters from thousands of supportive fans. Both Paris and her mother had nightmares as a result of the experience.

But had the wild, carefree party girl really reformed? Although she'd talked about cutting down before, it seemed as if jail had given her a new perspective: "I realized that there [are] a lot more important things in life and a lot more things to do," she admitted to King. "And I'm frankly sick of it. You know, I've been going out for a long time now. And yes, it's fun, but it's not going to be the mainstay of my life anymore."[21]

During the Walters interview, she'd mentioned working in the fields of breast cancer research, which maternal grandmother "Big Kathy" had died of; or possibly even multiple sclerosis, which ran in her father's family. She told King that she hoped to set up a transitional home for the other women prisoners who lack her advantages: "I know I can make a difference and hopefully stop this vicious circle of these people going in and out of jail."[22]

Paris's hoped-for halfway house and research efforts never saw the light of day, although she has since been involved in fund-raising efforts for both of the above illnesses as well as various animal rights and rescue causes, among others. And as a result of her jail time, she was dropped by the Endeavor talent agency, which had represented her since 2005, as well as by a few other clients.

But while Paris had been burned, she was hardly a burnout. "Even when she's using that cooey little baby voice, you can see the wheels turning in her head," social critic and author Michael Musto has remarked. Although "she pretends she doesn't care—the bad press bothers her" as it would most people. "But it also makes her steelier in her determination to get to the next level and prove everybody wrong."[23] As she was just about to do.

NOTES

1. David K. Li and Lucas Alpert, "Paris Hilton's Prison Warning," *Daily Telegraph* (May 7, 2007), www.dailytelegraph.com.au/news/paris-hiltons-prison-warning/story-e6freuy9–1111113485010.

2. Chas Newkey-Burden, *Paris Hilton: Life on the Edge* (London: John Blake, 2007), 235.

3. Sara Hammel, "Paris Hilton Is Dreading Jail Time," People.com (May 30, 2007), Paris Hilton, www.people.com/people/article/0,,20040643,00.html.

4. Rebecca Hardy, "So, Mrs. Hilton, Are You Ashamed of Your Daughter?" *Daily Mail* (London) (May 23, 2008): 15.

5. Mike Fleeman and Ken Lee, "Tears and Solitude for Paris Hilton in Jail," People.com (June 6, 2007), www.people.com/people/article/0,,20041406_20041492,00.html.

6. Michelle Tauber, Bob Meadows, Ken Lee, et al., "Law & Disorder," *People* 67, 25 (May 25, 2007), electronic database access [Proquest].

7. Ibid.

8. Michael Blood, "Early Release Just Latest Controversy for Baca," Associated Press (June 8, 2007), www.dailynews.com/ci_6098443.6.

9. Rocky Degadillo, "Paris Hilton Back to Jail?" (n.d.), www.theinsider.com/news/216395_Paris_Hilton_Back_to_Jail.

10. "Interview with Paris Hilton," CNN *Larry King Live* (June 27, 2007), transcripts.cnn.com/TRANSCRIPTS/0706/27/lkl.01.html.

11. Ibid.

12. Ken Lee and Lycia Naff, "Sheriff: Paris Hilton Was 'Deteriorating' in Jail," People.com (June 8, 2007), www.people.com/people/article/0,,20041406_20041858,00.html.

13. Hardy, "So, Mrs. Hilton."

14. Ibid.

15. Michelle Tauber, Bob Meadows, Ken Lee, et al., "Law & Disorder."

16. Hardy, "So, Mrs. Hilton."

17. Barbara Walters, "Hilton Calls Barbara Walters from Jail—'God Has Released Me,'" ABC News (June 11, 2007), abcnews.go.com/US/story?id=3264588&page=1.

18. CNN *Larry King Live*.

19. Hardy, "So, Mrs. Hilton."

20. Ibid.

21. Ibid.

22. CNN *Larry King Live*.

23. *Paris, Not France*, directed by Adria Petty, documentary (New York: MTV, 2008), unpublished transcript.

Chapter 7

FUTURE'S SO BRIGHT SHE'S GONNA WEAR SHADES— AND DESIGN THEM!

Like the city that bears her name, Paris will always cast a special light. Since her release from jail, she has worked diligently to upgrade her image while retaining her trademark joie de vivre. "I am a social person. I love to dance, I love to go out, I love music," she has said. "But a lot of people don't know that I'm a business person" including her acting/reality TV career, fashion line, album, and bestselling books, among other enterprises.[1] And she earns her own money, taking pride in the fact that she pays her own bills and has purchased her own home and cars. That's a lot more than many 20-somethings can say, some of who still depend on their families for financial support and even live with their parents.

ICON AND HUMANITARIAN

In fact, Paris has become somewhat of an icon. In 2009, her words were immortalized in the new edition of the *Oxford Dictionary of Quotations*—not "That's hot," or "Are you taping this?" but "Dress cute wherever you go, life is too short to blend in." This put her right alongside Confucius, Stephen Hawking, and President Barack Obama, who weighed in a bit more profoundly with, "The arc of history is long but it bends toward justice." Although more than 20,000 new quotations were added to the 65-year-old tome, it gave Paris that dollop of extra credibility that she seems to crave.

Her peers have also noticed that she's a force to be reckoned with. Shortly before she died at age 30 in January 2010 from complications from diabetes and self-neglect, Casey Johnson of the Johnson & Johnson fortune expressed envy of her childhood friend's success: Although "I love [Paris] . . . I hate that she has everything and everything has gone her way."[2] She neglected to consider, of course how hard Paris worked at her various undertakings, not to mention the many stumbling blocks and critics she has encountered along the way. Both Hilton sisters had remained close to the late heiress throughout the years; Nicky was even godmother to her adopted daughter, Ava. "Casey . . . had a big heart and she was a good friend," Paris observed. "I feel so sad; I don't want to believe it."[3]

Taking a cue from her mother Kathy, who has always been an active fund-raiser, Paris has become more involved with various charitable causes, starting with the annual jumble sale held at the Hilton estate at the Hamptons, in which family and friends sell cast-off clothes and other household goods and donate the proceeds to charity. She's supported various nonprofits such as Children's Hospital Los Angeles, Education Africa, Feeding America, Make-A-Wish Foundation, and many others. Most recently, she was named celebrity ambassador for "Songs for Soldiers," a charity whose goal is to provide active-duty military personnel in Afghanistan or Iraq with mp3 music players loaded with popular tunes donated by recording artists.

Paris even got political during the 2008 presidential campaign when she appeared in a "Funny or Die" video. Directed by Adam McKay, the 1 minute, 50 second clip shows Paris refuting then-presidential candidate John McCain's comparison of rival Barack Obama's leadership ability and knowledge of energy policy to that of celebrities such as herself and Britney Spears. In the video, Paris, clad in a leopard-print swimsuit and heels, starts out by suggesting that the personal mention by McCain must now mean that she was now a candidate in the presidential race, drawing similarities between her lifestyle and that of the president's, further qualifying her for the White House. She then goes on, in the manner of an academic speaker, to provide a reasoned and rational compromise for the U.S. energy crisis, combining elements of the policies from both candidates.

The video went viral with seven million hits and even had political commentators and heavyweights such as Speaker of the House Nancy Pelosi and Congressman Michael Burgess discussing the pros and cons of the "Paris compromise solution" and spawned a sequel, "Paris Hilton Gets Presidential with Martin Sheen," in which she interviews Martin Sheen about various political issues, seeking his advice as fictional president of *The West Wing* TV show.

One thing Paris has always been a champion of is animals, whether as pets or for other uses. A strong advocate of animal rights and in conjunction with the Humane Society of the United States (HSUS), she made sure that her Dollhouse line of women's clothing was fur-free. She completely stopped wearing fur in 2007 after watching a graphic video about treatment of animals used for manufacturing purposes and has periodically claimed to be a vegetarian ever since. (Perhaps the burger stop that eventually resulted in her incarceration also had an influence as well.)

MODEL, PRODUCER, ENTERTAINER

But her "meat and potatoes," so to speak, remains the entertainment industry, including the successful, highly rated *My New BFF* TV shows that she produced, created, and starred in on MTV. The shows chronicle Paris's lifelong search for a "bestie" with whom she could share her hopes, dreams, and cute clothes (if a female), weeding out what she herself has called "Paris-ites," those who want to use her fame and notoriety to further their own careers. The winner would have the honor of participating in Paris's privileged, glamorous life, traveling with her to parties, openings, or wherever else she appeared. The concept was so appealing that in 2009 Paris was nominated for the Teen Choice Awards for female Choice Reality/Variety TV Star and the show itself as Choice TV Show—Reality/Variety. That same year she won a Fox Reality Award for "Innovator of Reality TV." Paris has repeatedly stated that she's planning a BFF show franchise in the United States and abroad.

Starting with the season one premiere on September 30, 2008, 16 women and 2 men competed in clever and often Machiavellian challenges that pitted one against the other in true reality show tradition, including a 24-hour party marathon, a contest to pick the biggest "fake" in the house, and a lie detector test administered by entertainer and TV/radio host Ryan Seacrest. Each week, Paris eliminated one (or more) contestants and selected a different "pet" who served as her eyes and ears and to whom she sent text messages to about various events. While aspiring rocker Brittany Flickinger emerged the winner, the "BFF" label didn't quite stick, and a few months later they parted ways. "All that girl wanted was the free trips, the goodie bags, staying at Paris' mansion and the parties and clubs," observed one insider, who sounded suspiciously like mom Kathy. "She was desperate for money. She was another one of these girls using Paris to get famous. We've seen it happen a million times."[4] Thus, another Paris-ite was squashed.

Or as Paris more tactfully put it in a statement to the press, "I loved her and I trusted her, but sometimes people get too caught up and they change." Who did emerge as of a fixture in the BFF universe was eliminated season one contestant Onch, a supposed artist and designer, dubbed a "life pet" by Paris. Onch appeared in subsequent BFF shows exhibiting his real talent—stirring up drama by spreading rumors and innuendo from one BFF aspirant to the next.

Season two, also on MTV, premiered on June 2, 2009, and included 13 women and 3 men. Natalie Reid, a professional Paris look-alike, made a special guest appearance as Paris while the real heiress slipped into a disguise and pretended to be contestant, mingling anonymously with the other contenders. Challenges included hosting a dinner for Paris's friends and family, a stint in a "prison" with Paris clad in sexy garb as the jailer/ judge, and a grilling—as in being asked questions, not actually roasted—*National-Enquirer* style from a reporter. This time a male, Stephen Hampton, was chosen, and his Twitter page still features photos of him with Paris.

Other BFF shows have been filmed abroad. In the UK, *Paris Hilton's British Best Friend* premiered on January 29, 2009, on ITV2. Most of the series was shot in London, and 12 women and 1 man competed, with the male Sam Hextall winning the competition (is there a pattern here?). Shooting for *Paris Hilton's Dubai BFF* filmed in the United Arab Emirates (U.A.E.) began in June 2009 and as of this writing is in post-production. There's no doubt a female will emerge a winner, since all of the 20 contestants are women, half from the Middle East, half from elsewhere but currently residing in Dubai. The series also filmed Paris's reactions to the region, which she'd never visited before. Paris on a camel is definitely better PR than Paris smoking one.

However, sometimes controversy still follows her. Her 2008 film *The Hottie and the Nottie* garnered excruciatingly bad reviews and her second "Golden Raspberry" (the first was for the 2005 *House of Wax*) along with being featured on several "worst of" 2008 movie lists and being considered by many sources to be one of the most awful movies ever made. It was a major box office bomb, grossing less than $30,000 during opening week and costing the production company over $8 million. Billed as a romantic comedy and revolving around a young man's childhood crush on the "hottie" (Paris) and her hideously ugly best friend, the failed Cinderella plot turned out to be an exercise in bad taste. However, it was released in the UK, made into a DVD, and aired several times on the "Bravo" TV channel, proving that for some people, even a spectacularly failed Paris is better than no Paris at all.

In early 2010, a film ad for Devassa (Portuguese for "very blonde") beer aired in Brazil, featuring Paris in a tight black dress running a

Actress Paris Hilton arrives at the Los Angeles premiere of The Hottie and the Nottie *in the Hollywood section of Los Angeles, February 4, 2008. (AP Photo/ Chris Weeks)*

cold can of beer down her body in front of a window, in full view of a photographer in a neighboring building as a crowd gathered on the street to watch. Presumably too hot to handle for consumers in a culture that boasts topless beaches and bikini waxes, the clip was deemed both overly sexy and sexist by watchdog groups and the Brazilian government and was pulled off the air. But it undoubtedly sold lots of product, and that's what Paris is all about—or at least the image that she projects. Paris also appeared in *The Other Guys*, a police comedy starring Samuel L. Jackson, Will Ferrell, and Mark Wahlberg, which was released in 2010.

PARIS THE SINGER

Paris first announced plans to record an album in 2003 and founded Heiress Records, a label of Warner Bros., a year later. She released her debut album, *Paris*, on August 22, 2006. The album reached number six on the Billboard 200 for a week, with the first single, "Stars Are Blind," being a Top 10 hit in 17 countries. Although reviews were mixed, many were positive, ranging from "You may hate what she stands for, but don't let that keep you off the dance floor" (*Entertainment Weekly*) to "An enjoyable pop romp" (*Billboard*) to the somewhat snarkier "Like cotton candy, the food group she most resembles, what may seem like a mouthful for a moment is gone in the blink of an eye, leaving a sweet aftertaste and empty calories behind" (*Los Angeles Times*).

Also in August 2006, British graffiti artist Banksy and a music producer known as "Danger Mouse" waged guerrilla warfare on Paris's debut album, replacing some 500 copies of it in British music stores with an altered mockery. Along with a completely reworked cover and liner notes that included topless photos of Paris, there were remixes of her songs (credited to "DM" aka Danger Mouse) with titles such as "Why Am I Famous," "What Have I Done," and "What Am I For." When asked "why?" the two came up with the somewhat mystifying response, "It's hard to improve on perfection, but we had to try."[5] The copies were quickly removed and replaced with originals, proving once again that while there's no such thing as bad PR, sometimes it can be confusing.

In addition to a speaking part, Paris also provided songs to the musical *Repo! The Genetic Opera* (2008), directed by Darren Lynn Bousman. Touted as *Rocky Horror* meets *Blade Runner*, the rock opera /musical revolves around a biotech company that launches an organ-financing program with terms similar to a standard car loan, with—no surprise here—dire consequences. Director Bousman observed, "We gave her some music and said, 'You have one day to come back and perform this.' She came back the next day, memorized everything, was pitch-perfect . . . she was awesome."[6]

In July 2007 she announced that she was working on a new, as yet untitled album and in 2008 released two singles, "My BFF" and "Paris for President." Although she claims to have written and finished all the songs and will be using her label Heiress Records, the second album has yet to be released.

AS AN AUTHOR

In the spring of 2004, she published an autobiographical book, *Confessions of an Heiress: A Tongue-in-Chic Peek Behind the Pose*, from Fireside Press, cowritten with Merle Ginsberg, which includes full color photographs of her and her advice on life as an heiress (see appendix A for a list of popular "Paris-isms"). She reportedly received a $100,000 advance for this book and, unlike other celebrities, actually earned it back. While some critics panned it as amateurish and the book was parodied on David Letterman, it became a *New York Times* bestseller. In 2005, she followed it up with a designer diary, *Your Heiress Diary: Confess It All to Me*, also from Fireside and with Ginsberg, featuring photos of Paris and her pithy observations. And of course Tinkerbell had her own bestseller, *The Tinkerbell Hilton Diaries*, published in 2004 by Grand Central (see page XX). Paris has often mentioned that she reads a lot and frequently writes in her journal, although unlike BFF Nicole Richie, who penned *The Truth about Diamonds* (Harper, 2006), she has not attempted a novel. At least not yet.

PARIS THE ENTREPRENEUR

Paris makes it easy to find out what she's selling these days: along with her own Web site, www.parishilton.com, which serves as a promotional and advertising platform for all products Paris, fan-based Web sites such as www.parishiltonsite.net and www.parishiltononline.net reveals an almost dizzying array of her namesake offerings, most of which are available in stores and online. These include perfumes (for both men

and women), handbags, sunglasses, shoes, sportswear, and hair acces-
sories, including Dream Catchers Clipin-Go Hair Extensions, so, according to www.parishiltonsite.net, "you can have the EXACT same
hair as Paris . . . Quick and easy—a full head application takes only
2½ hours [and] Does NOT damage the client's own hair—REALLY,"
and the simpler and perhaps less risky Bandit, basically a hairpiece with
several interchangeable scarves.

Her most recent perfume and 10th scent, Tease, was released in
May 2010, establishing Paris as a force to be reckoned with in that
industry. She posed as a mermaid and channeled Tinkerbell in past
fragrance campaigns and for Tease went for the old-school Hollywood
siren look. "I got to dress up like my idol Marilyn Monroe," she observed. "Tease is a really sweet and flirty scent, so the name is very
fitting. It's playful and sexy–perfect for grabbing attention."[7] At $55
a bottle it's a bit more than a casual trifling with the pocketbook; according to The Wall Street Journal, her partnership with Parlux fragrance, the manufacturer and distributor for her perfumes, has reaped
a wholesale revenue of about $100 million.[8] Products are sold in retail
outlets ranging from Perfumania to Macy's to JC Penney and include
customers in more than 80 countries.

Along with fragrances by Paris, Parlux also distributes a cornucopia
of Paris watches for all occasions, seasons, and moods from a casual
chronograph to a dressier bracelet, adorned with all manner of her
trademark glitz, in shades of mostly pink and in a variety of shapes and
sizes, with prices ranging from $50 to $150.

But wait . . . as the TV infomercial says, there's more! Along with
Paris's "Little Lilly" couture for the fashion-forward lap dog, Paris
launched a "Creativity" collection for budding scrapbookers and artists. Her most recent project, tentatively scheduled for release some-
time in 2010, is a line of lingerie and swimwear. It will include "panties
and bras, bikinis and cover-ups [to] flatter and enhance," according the
Parishilton.com Web site. The bra will boost more than Paris's financial assets: "I designed [it] for flat-chested girls and it makes your boobs
look huge!" she observed. "People think it's fake boobs. Everyone's like,
'Did you . . . ?' I'm like, 'No!' It makes me look like a double-D. I'm
flat-chested compared to most girls in Hollywood."[9] Rather than go the
surgical enhancement route of many of her peers, as is typical of her,
Paris forged her own path and avoided potentially dangerous surgery.

The majority of the items fall in the mid-price range, making them affordable for young women. Paris seems to know her target audience and presents the various items in a fun, appealing, and yet tastefully glamorous way. "I'm an actress, a brand, a businesswoman," she has often said. "I'm all kinds of stuff." And she sells it all, too.

PARIS AND PEREZ

Paris has even served as a muse for Mario Armando Lavandeira Jr., the infamous celebrity blogger who reinvented himself as Perez Hilton. Purveyor of what many consider to be Hollywood's most hated Web site and sometimes accused of being biased and controversial, Perez has remained good friends with Paris, the source of his nickname and frequent subject of his posts, even appearing on her BFF TV show.

Along with speaking out against discriminatory behavior against certain celebrities (and seemingly randomly and gratuitously attacking

Paris Hilton, left, and Perez Hilton during Perez Hilton's 31st birthday bash held at the Viper Room in West Hollywood on March 28, 2009. (Katy Winn/AP Images for Perez Hilton)

others whom he dislikes), Perez has been criticized for not reporting negative or unflattering stories or rumors about his namesake; for example siding against Doug Reinhardt during the recent breakup with Paris, calling him "Douchey Doug" while Paris's old-yet-new-again companion Jason Shaw is "her hottie of an ex." "Oh, and as for those rumors that Douchey D supposedly spent $2 million of his own money on Paris, her friends are calling BS on that!" dishes Perez. "In fact, sources tell us the douchebag would pressure Paris to split her appearance fees with him, when no one could care less if he showed up or not!"[10]

Perez's pipeline of information and gossip runs wide and deep, and while he sometimes grossly misinforms, such as when he erroneously reported the death of Cuban President Fidel Castro in 2007, he is a force to be reckoned with, at least in the rumor-and-innuendo-filled world of celebrity gossip.

BREAK-INS, BREAK-UPS, OH MY!

While Paris is pretty much single these days after her breakup with Doug Reinhardt, she's often said she's dreamed of a white wedding, a husband, and children. However, the heiress is exhibiting her practical side by waiting for the right guy to come along, even though she will be 30 in 2011. But as with many young women of her generation she is in no hurry, realizing that she still has plenty of time and many worlds to conquer.

And she continues to struggle with the downside of celebrity, including being the target of criminals. In 2005, a teenager from Massachusetts (not named because he was a minor) was sentenced to 11 months in a juvenile facility for hacking into Paris's T-Mobile account and posting her and her celebrity friends' phone numbers on the Internet, among other serious but unrelated transgressions. Consequently, a good portion of young Hollywood had to change their phone numbers.

In February 2006, when Paris was moving from one house to another, a storage locker where she and Nicky had stashed personal items was suddenly "liberated" because of a supposedly unpaid bill. The owner of the storage facility seized the items and sold them to Phoenix-based broker David Hans Schmidt, who planned to auction them off for

$20 million. According to Schmidt, who is infamous for his ties to the celebrity porn industry, "the items include 18 diaries whose pages recount Hilton's sexual dalliances, celebrity encounters and other adventures; photographs of Hilton in a number of locales, such as St. Tropez, and 'wild parties' on yachts and in private homes; as well as her computers, clothing, videos and furniture."[11]

Not surprisingly, some things surfaced a few months later on a now-defunct Web site, parisexposed.com. For $39.97, anyone could view her bank records, personal diaries and home videos. The Hiltons filed a lawsuit against Nabil and Nabila Haniss of Culver City, CA, who paid $2,775 for the bounty—apparently Schmidt must have changed his mind about exploiting it for himself—and then allegedly sold them for $10 million to entrepreneur Bardia Persa, creator of Parisexposed.com. The site was eventually shut down, although periodically some of the personal information still appears on the Internet, not to mention a number of illicit images that have been doctored.

Then on December 20, 2008, at around 4 A.M., a man in a hooded sweater and gloves entered Paris's Sherman Oaks home and stole $2 million worth of jewelry and other items from her bedroom. Fortunately Paris was out at the time and no one was injured. "I'm just happy that she's okay," stated Kathy, adding that she and Paris agreed that "really, it is just stuff."[12] And on August 24, 2010, yet another would-be burglar was foiled with the help of current squeeze Cy Waits. While Paris tweeted that a man with two large knives was trying to get into her home and called 911, Waits allegedly went downstairs with his gun to check it out, found the intruder, Nathan Parada, and told him to drop the knives and get on his stomach, pointing the gun at him until the police arrived. If convicted, Parada could face up to six years in prison.[13] Although Paris has frequently said that such things upset her and make her feel violated, she remains determined to move forward no matter what. "Every time something bad happens I just pick myself up and just go again.[14]

"I don't want to be known as the granddaughter of the Hiltons. I want to be known as Paris," she has often remarked. So the next time you see Paris Hilton on *The Late Show with David Letterman* or another TV, radio, or other media outlet and she giggles and vamps "Huge" or "That's hot!" remember that she's probably cooking up her next big project. "It's funny, people don't think I don't know what's going on but I always do," she observes. She has learned a lot playing, for a lack of a better word, dumb. "People show more of their cards because they don't think I'm realizing what's going on."[15]

If anything, the opposite is true. "People think this was all given to me—it wasn't," she sums up. "It was all me, working very, very hard. Wherever I travel I'm always working. Even if I go somewhere for fun, I end up having to work." But she's hardly complaining: "I'm doing what I love. It's amazing . . . A great life."[16]

NOTES

1. Ani Esmailian, "Casey Johnson Was Jealous of Paris Hilton" (Jan. 13, 2010), www.hollyscoop.com/casey-johnson/casey-johnson-was-jealous-of-paris-hilton_22728.aspx#ixzz0mJFPTwbH.

2. Ibid.

3. Bridget Daly, "Paris Reacts to Casey Johnson's Death" (Jan. 5, 2010), www.hollyscoop.com/paris-hilton/paris-reacts-to-casey-johnsons-death_22641.aspx#ixzz0mJFnDLHa.

4. "Paris Hilton and Brittany Flickinger: BFFs No More" (n.d.), www.celebrity-gossip.net/celebrities/hollywood/paris-hilton-and-brittany-flickinger-bffs-no-more-212388.

5. "Danger Mouse, Banksy Burn Paris," Spin.com (Sept. 5, 2006), www.spin.com/articles/danger-mouse-banksy-burn-paris.

6. Nicole Powers, "Darren Lynn Bousman: Repossessed" (Nov. 7, 2008), suicidegirls.com/interviews/Darren+Lynn+Bousman3A+Repossessed.

7. Marissa Patlingrao Cooley, reporting by Katherine Kluznik Rentmeester (*People* magazine) "Paris' 10th Fragrance 'Tease' Featured in People," Parishilton.com Web site (June 24, 2010), parishilton.com/news.

8. "Walkabout New York," video interview with the *Wall Street Journal's* Lee Hawkins, Parishilton.com Web site (June 22, 2010), parishilton.com/news.

9. "Paris Hilton to Boost Assets with Lingerie Line," Contact Music (Jan. 21, 2010), http://www.contactmusic.com/news.nsf/story/hilton-to-boost-assets-with-lingerie-line_1129429.

10. Perez Hilton, "Paris Hilton Breaking News and Gossip," Perez Hilton.com (n.d.), perezhilton.com/category/paris-hilton/#ixzz0p G6U19jt.

11. Robert W. Welkos, "Treasures of Paris (Hilton) Offered for $20 Million," LAtimes.com (Feb. 3, 2006), articles.latimes.com/2006/ feb/03/local/me-paris3.

12. "Paris Hilton's Mother Talks about Break-In" (Dec. 2, 2008), www.thecelebritytruth.com/paris-hiltons-mother-talks-breakin/ 005376.

13. Nancy Dillon, "Paris Hilton's Boyfriend Cy Waits Pulled Gun On Knife-Wielding Home Intruder Nathan Parada," New York Daily News (Aug. 27, 2010), http://www.nydailynews.com/gossip/2010/08/ 27/2010-08-27_paris_hiltons_boyfriend_cy_waits_pulled_gun_on_ knifeweilding_home_intruder_natha.html.

14. *Paris, Not France*, directed by Adria Petty, documentary (New York: MTV, 2008), unpublished transcript.

15. Ibid.

16. Ibid.

Appendix A

THE QUOTABLE PARIS

That's hot!

The only rule is don't be boring.

I got my eye on you boy, and when I get my eye on something, it's like search and destroy.—"Not Leaving Without You," from the album *Paris*

It hurts that, you know, the media's made me into sort of this like punching bag or cartoon character—they think that I don't have any feelings, and, you know, it hurts like anyone else.—TMZ interview, July 19, 2006

A lot of women feel it's a man's world. Some people think all you need to do is marry a rich guy, and you don't need to do anything with your life. . . . I would hate that. I don't care whether he has money or he doesn't, because I don't need it, and that's a good feeling that I don't have to worry about that.—*Guardian Unlimited*, July 8, 2006

I'm an actress, a brand, a businesswoman. I'm all kinds of stuff.

Every woman should have four pets in her life. A mink in her closet, a jaguar in her garage, a tiger in her bed, and a jackass who pays for everything.[1]

Dress cute wherever you go, life is too short to blend in.

I don't want to be known as the granddaughter of the Hiltons.

I want to be known as Paris.

I'm judged because of something that an ex-boyfriend did to me. I'm not a slut at all. I've only had a few boyfriends. And I don't even do anything with anyone—it's just the media making stuff up . . . I'm far less promiscuous than any of my friends.—TMZ interview, July 19, 2006

It's sexier when a girl is flirty but she doesn't do anything.—*Guardian Unlimited*, July 8, 2006

I'm totally normal. I think it's obnoxious when people demand limos or bodyguards. I eat at McDonald's or Taco Bell. My parents always taught us to be humble. We're not spoiled.

At parties, everyone always thinks I'm drinking—but actually I rarely drink. I live on energy drinks, basically. I LOVE Vitamin Water. I have cases in my house. I drink energy drinks and Vitamin Water all night. That's how I manage to stay up late and never smudge my makeup or mess up my hair. You can see all these girls leaving a party at the end of the night, and they look terrible because they were too out of it to reapply their makeup or even glance in a mirror. This is a huge mistake. People remember how you look when you leave as much as they remember how you looked when you arrived.

I don't enjoy going out anymore. . . . It's such a pain. It's everyone saying, "Let's do a deal! Can I have a picture?" I'm just, like, "These people are such losers. I can't believe I used to love doing this."—OXNews.com, June 14, 2005

No matter what a woman looks like, if she's confident, she's sexy.

People are going to judge me: "Paris Hilton, she uses money to get what she wants." Whatever, I haven't accepted money from my parents since I was 18. I've worked my ass off. I have things no heiress has. I've done it all on my own, like a hustler.—*Los Angeles Times*, Aug. 18, 2006

I haven't seen it, but when people copy you, that's like the most flattering thing, so whatever people can say, I just laugh about it. It doesn't matter to me.—On *South Park*: "Stupid Spoiled Whore Video Playset #8.12," 2004

If you have a beautiful face you don't need big fake boobs to get anyone's attention.

It's traditional for an heiress to be raised in a sheltered way. No one thinks that's true of me, but it actually was.

This is Earth. Isn't it hot?

All British people have plain names, and that works pretty well over there.

It will work. I am a marketing genius.

I'd imagine my wedding as a fairy tale . . . huge, beautiful, and white.

I didn't want to be like all these socialites—they sit at home, and go to the debutante ball, and marry some rich guy and that's it. That's all they do. I wanted to do my own thing so I could buy whatever I want, do whatever I want.

I first wanted to be a veterinarian. And then I realized you had to give them shots to put them to sleep, so I decided I'd just buy a bunch of animals and have them in my house instead.—*Guardian Unlimited*, July 8, 2006

I take my dog Tinkerbell seriously. I take my job seriously. But I don't take myself all that seriously.

There's nobody in the world like me. I think every decade has an iconic blonde—like Marilyn Monroe or Princess Diana—and right now, I'm that icon.—Yahoo News, July 17, 2006

People can't believe how hard I work. . . . I love it. I think it just runs through my veins. My great-grandfather was a bellboy and had a dream to do a hotel chain, so I think I get it from him.—*Guardian Unlimited*, July 8, 2006

You need to look like a lady at the Oscars. Otherwise, Joan Rivers will tear you apart. Then again, you aren't really anyone till Joan Rivers tears you apart. So wait until you are someone, then dress like a lady at the Oscars.—*Confessions of an Heiress*

I just read some story online that I demanded lobsters on a movie set. So ridiculous, people make up the silliest stories sometimes. Oh well.—Twitter, Oct. 19, 2009

Not every heiress is famous. Or fun. There are a lot of boring heiresses out there.

I used to act dumb. That act is no longer cute. Now, I would like to make a difference . . . God has given me this new chance.—To Barbara Walters via phone from LA County Jail, where she served prison sentence for traffic violations.

I play dumb like Jessica Simpson plays dumb. But we know exactly what we're doing. We're smart blondes.—Yahoo News, July 17, 2006

I'm not like that smart. I like forget stuff all the time.—Law enforcement interview, Sept. 23, 2006

I really don't think; I just walk.

Who are you wearing?

The root of all evil is not money, it's boredom.

I desperately hate one thing about my body. I have size 11 feet. Yeah, it sucks, because I see all these super cute shoes in the stores: Guccis, YSLs, Manolos. And when they bring them out in my size, they look like clown shoes.

If you want to make the camera your friend, pretend it's a cute boy!

One of my heroes is Barbie. She may not do anything, but she always looks great doing it.

I'd rather not do anything. Guys want you more when you don't. Young girls should know that.—Post Chronicle, Dec. 15, 2006

Someone told me you start liking sex when you hit 30—but we'll see.—Post Chronicle, Jan. 6, 2007

I turn down perverted things, some sex things. Like a Paris Hilton blow-up doll . . . They were like, "They'll sell for $50,000 each, it'll be the real-life you." And I'm like, "I really don't want a real-life me with anyone, anywhere."—No!, Glam Network, Jan. 5, 2007

I've only done it with, like, a couple of boyfriends. People think I sleep with everyone, but I'm not like that. I like kissing, but that's all I do. I'm not having sex for a year, I've decided. I'll kiss but nothing else.—GQ magazine, Aug. 2006

I just do little jokes all the time and people think I'm serious. I know exactly who Gordon Ramsay is, I know exactly who Gordon Brown is . . . I just say jokes but they think I'm serious which I think is funny and I think I kind of play up the image sometimes because—whatever—it's just entertainment.—*Daily Mail*, Jan. 28, 2009

Wal-mart . . . do they like make walls there?—*The Simple Life*, 2003

There's a lot of advantages to being my best friend.—*London Telegraph*, Jan. 28, 2009

I'm the nicest, most loyal person in the world when it comes to my friends. I would really do almost anything to make sure they're happy. But I only want friends who are there for me just like I'm there for them. Otherwise it's too painful.

That wrinkly white-haired guy used me in his campaign ad, which means I'm running for president. So thanks for the endorsement white-haired dude, and I want America to know I'm, like, totally ready to lead.—Lampooning a John McCain U.S. presidential campaign video using her image, Aug. 2008

I loved all the Aaron Spelling shows, *Beverly Hills 90210* and *Models Inc.* At that time, I had pet rats I was raising and I always named all the baby rats after the characters in the shows.

When I was a kid I had no idea I lived in a mansion. Then I went to a friend's house and I was like—"Oh."

I like it, . . . but it's yellow, and I'm like, I didn't want yellow for my engagement ring.

I've had a lot of people in my past who were friends with me just to get publicity. When I was young, my mom or sister used to have to point out if someone was using me to make a name for themselves—you know, linking arms with me on the red carpet and trying to get in every picture. But now I can see for myself when someone is just hungry for attention.—*Fabulous Mag* interview, Jan. 2009

I have this great test to see if a girl's a real friend. When we're shopping I'll pick out an outfit that I know looks hot and one that is awful. If my friend says the bad one looks good, I know she's not a good friend.—*Fabulous Mag* interview, Jan. 2009

A true heiress is never mean to anyone—except a girl who steals your boyfriend.

You don't have to be an heiress to look like one; if you act like one then everyone will just presume you are one.

NOTE

1. Sources: *Confessions of an Heiress*, www.notablequotes.com, www.thinkexist.com, www.quotelucy.com, www.brainyquote.com, www.allgreatquotes.com.

Appendix B
FILM AND OTHER CREDITS

1992

Wishman (movie): Girl on Beach

1997

MuchOnDemand TV series: Herself—Guest (unknown episodes)

2000

MTV *Fashionably Loud: Spring Break, Cancun 2000* (TV): Herself—
   Audience (uncredited)

2001

Zoolander (movie): Herself
Young Hollywood Awards (TV): Herself

Source: The information in this appendix is from the Internet
Movie Database (www.imdb.com/name/nm0385296), MTV.com.

2002

QIK2JDG (movie): Strung-out Supermodel
Nine Lives (movie): Jo
America's Party: Live from Las Vegas (TV): Herself
Fashion File (TV): Herself
—"Mercedes-Benz Fashion Week" TV episode: Herself

2003

Acting:

Dr. Seuss' The Cat in the Hat:	Female Club-Goer
Wonderland:	Barbie
L.A. Knights:	Sadie
Pauly Shore Is Dead:	Herself

Documentary:

Playboy's 50th Anniversary Celebration (TV)
The Making of "Nine Lives" (Video)
It's Good to Be . . .
The Hilton Sisters, Queens of Making Money TV episode: Herself

Reality TV/Awards Shows/Special Appearances:

The Simple Life, Season 1
   "Ro-Day-O vs. Ro-Dee-O" (December 2, 2003): Herself
   "Dairy Farmin' Divas" (December 3, 2003): Herself
   "Sonic Burger Shenanigans" (December 9, 2003): Herself
   "The One About the Rumors" (December 16, 2003): Herself
   "Shopaholics" (December 17, 2003): Herself
Hollywood Squares (5 episodes, 2003)
   —TV episode dated May 16, 2003 (as the Hilton Sisters): Guest
      Appearance
   —TV episode dated May 15, 2003 (as the Hilton Sisters): Guest
      Appearance

—TV episode dated May 14, 2003 (as the Hilton Sisters): Guest Appearance
—TV episode dated May 13, 2003 (as the Hilton Sisters): Guest Appearance
—TV episode dated May 12, 2003 (as The Hilton Sisters): Guest Appearance
Saturday Night Live—Al Sharpton/Pink TV episode: Herself
The 2003 Billboard Music Awards (TV): Herself
Playboy's 50th Anniversary Celebration (TV): Herself
Tinseltown TV: Herself
—TV episode dated September 13, 2003: Herself
MTV Video Music Awards 2003 (TV): Herself
The Making of 'Nine Lives' (Video): Herself
2003 MTV Movie Awards (TV): Herself

2004

Acting:

Veronica Mars: Caitlin Ford (1 episode, 2004)
—"Credit Where Credit's Due" TV episode: Caitlin Ford
The Hillz: Heather Smith
Raising Helen: Amber
The O.C.: Kate (1 episode, 2004)
—"The L.A." TV episode: Kate
George Lopez: Ashley (1 episode, 2004)
—"Jason Tutors Max" TV episode: Ashley/Lorraine
Las Vegas: Madison (1 episode, 2004)
—"Things That Go Jump in the Night" TV episode: Madison
Win a Date with Tad Hamilton! (uncredited): Heather

Documentary:

Biography [Self]
—"Millionheirs" TV episode [Actress]
VH1 Big in 04 (TV) [Actress]
Making the Video [Self]
—"Eminem: Just Lose It" TV episode [Actress]

Fashion in Focus [Self]
   —"New Kids on the Block: Part 2" TV episode [Actress]
"1 Night in Paris": (Video) [Actress]
   aka "Paris Hilton Sex Tape"—USA (bootleg title)
Style Star [Self]
   —"Paris & Nicky Hilton" TV episode [Actress]
E! True Hollywood Story
   —"Trust Fund Babies" TV episode: Herself
The Most Shocking Celebrity Moments of 2004 (TV): Herself
Last Laugh '04 (TV): Herself
The Ultimate Hollywood Blonde: Herself
101 Biggest Celebrity Oops (TV): Herself—#65: "More Things They Shouldn't Have Said"
South Park: "Stupid Spoiled Whore Video Playset (#8.12)"

Reality TV/Awards Shows/Special Appearances:

The Simple Life, Season 1
   Episode 6: "Boy Crazy"—January 7, 2004
   Episode 7: "Goodbye and Good Luck"—January 14, 2004
   Episode 8: "The Reunion"—January 14, 2004
   Episode 9: "The Lost Episode"—January 26, 2004
The Simple Life 2: Road Trip
   "Mermaid Outing" (June 16, 2004): Herself
   "The Journey Begins" (June 16, 2004): Herself
   "Nudist Resort" (June 23, 2004): Herself
   "Making Sausages" (June 30, 2004): Herself
   "Jenny's First Date" (July 7, 2004): Herself
   "Dancing Sheep" (July 14, 2004): Herself
   "Play Ball" (July 21, 2004): Herself
   "Brand New Look" (July 28, 2004): Herself
   "Back in the Saddle" (August 4, 2004): Herself
   "Deputized" (August 4, 2004): Herself
   "The Stuff We Weren't Allowed to Show You" (November 17, 2004): Herself
Bullrun: Cops, Cars & Superstars TV series [Actress]
The Teen Choice Awards 2004 (TV) [Actress]
2004 MTV Movie Awards (TV) [Actress]

2005

Acting:

House of Wax: Paige Edwards
American Dreams: Barbara Eden
    —"California Dreamin'" TV episode: Barbara Eden
Wetten, dass . . . ?: Herself
    —"Wetten, dass . . . ? aus Aspendos" TV episode: Herself

Documentary:

Celebrity News Reels Presents: Best of Paris (Video) [Actress]
    aka *Best of Paris*—International (English title)
101 Sexiest Celebrity Bodies (TV): Herself—place #101
See Paris Die!: Herself
The Secret Map of Hollywood: Herself
E! True Hollywood Story
    —"The Hilton Sisters" TV episode: Herself

Producer:

The Simple Life (16 episodes, 2005)

Reality TV/Awards Shows/Special Appearances:

The Simple Life 3: Interns
    "Mechanics" (January 26, 2005): Herself
    "Secretary" (January 26, 2005): Herself
    "Airline" (February 9, 2005): Herself
    "Mortuary" (February 16, 2005): Herself
    "Plastic Surgery" (February 23, 2005): Herself
    "Broadcasting" (March 2, 2005): Herself
    "Daycare" (March 9, 2005): Herself
    "Zoo" (March 16, 2005): Herself
    "Culinary" (March 23, 2005): Herself
    "Psychic" (March 30, 2005): Herself
    "Nursing Home" (April 6, 2005): Herself
    "Ad Agency" (April 13, 2005): Herself
    "Firefighters" (April 20, 2005): Herself

"Manufacturing" (April 28, 2005): Herself
"Dentistry" (May 12, 2005): Herself
"Wedding Planner" (May 12, 2005): Herself
2005 Radio Music Awards (TV): Herself
2005 American Music Awards (TV): Herself—Presenter
    aka *The 33rd Annual American Music Awards*—USA (series title)
Playboy: Hef's Halloween Spooktacular (Video) [Actress]
MTV Video Music Awards 2005 (TV): Herself—Presenter
The Teen Choice Awards 2005 (TV): Herself—Attendee
I Want to Be a Hilton: Herself (1 episode, 2005)
    —TV episode #1.2: Herself
Saturday Night Live—Paris Hilton/Keane, TV episode: Herself—Host/Various
The Girls Next Door: Herself
    —"A Midsummer Night's Dream" TV episode (uncredited): Herself

2006

Acting:

Pledge This!: Victoria English
    aka *National Lampoon's Pledge This!*—USA (complete title)
Bottoms Up (Video): Lisa Mancini

Documentary:

Forbes Celebrity 100: Who Made Bank? (TV): Herself
Rock Legends: Platinum Weird (TV): Herself
Bucht der Milliardäre (TV): Herself
This Is Paris (TV) [Actress]
Overrated in '06 (TV): Herself
Video on Trial
    —TV episode #2.9: Herself—Accused

Producing:

Pledge This! (executive producer)
    aka *National Lampoon's Pledge This!*

Reality TV/Awards Shows/Special Appearances:

The Simple Life 4: Til Death Do Us Part
  "The Nolan Family" (June 4, 2006): Herself
  "The Ghauri Family" (June 11, 2006): Herself
  "The Weekes Family" (June 18, 2006): Herself
  "The Padilla Family" (June 25, 2006): Herself
  "Bowden Family" (July 9, 2006): Herself
  "Murrie Family" (July 16, 2006): Herself
  "Contreras Family" (July 23, 2006): Herself
  "Beggs Family" (July 30, 2006): Herself
  "Burton Family" (August 6, 2006): Herself
  "The Confrontation" (August 13, 2006): Herself
Arby's Action Sports Awards (TV): Herself
VH1 Big in 06 Awards (TV): Herself
The 2006 World Music Awards (TV): Herself
2006 American Music Awards (TV): Herself—Presenter
40 Dumbest Celeb Quotes . . . Ever (TV): Herself
MTV Video Music Awards 2006 (TV): Herself—Presenter
The Girls Next Door: Herself
  —"Here's Looking at You, Hef" TV episode: Herself
  —"A Midsummer Night's Dream" (2005) TV episode (uncred-
    ited): Herself
2006 MuchMusic Video Awards (TV): Herself—Presenter
Popworld: Herself (1 episode, 2006)
  —TV episode dated February 18, 2006: Herself
Top of the Pops: Reloaded: Herself (1 episode, 2006)
  —TV episode dated February 18, 2006: Herself
Brit Awards 2006 (TV): Herself—Presenter

2007

Acting:

Stories USA: Sadie (segment "L.A. Knights")

Documentary:

America the Beautiful [Actress]
Celebrity A-List Bloopers (TV): Herself

Reality TV/Awards Shows/Special Appearances:

The Simple Life 5: Goes to Camp
  "Welcome to Camp Shawnee" (May 28, 2007): Herself
  "Big Primpin'" (June 6, 2007): Herself
  "Pageant Girls Just Want to Have Fun" (June 10, 2007): Herself
  "Showstoppers" (June 17, 2007): Herself
  "Flirting with Disaster" (June 24, 2007): Herself
  "Committed" (July 1, 2007): Herself
  "Say Hello to Myke Hawke" (July 8, 2007): Herself
  "Babes in the Woods" (July 22, 2007): Herself
  "Almost Fame-Less" (July 29, 2007): Herself
  "Hollywood Ending" (August 5, 2007): Herself
TMZ on TV: Herself (1 episode, 2007)
  —TV episode #1.9: Herself
What Perez Sez: Herself (1 episode, 2007)
  —"About the VMAs" TV episode: Herself
MTV VMA Pre Show Royale (TV): Herself
2007 MTV Movie Awards (TV): Herself
America's Next Top Model: Herself (1 episode, 2007)
  —"The Girl Who Gets Thrown in the Pool" TV episode: Herself

Thanks:

Heckler (special thanks)
"Lindsay Fully Loaded" (Video) (special thanks)
Born into Mafia (special thanks)
"Paris in Jail: The Music Video" (Video) (special thanks)

2008

Acting:

Repo! The Genetic Opera: Amber Sweet
The Hottie & the Nottie: Cristabel Abbott
An American Carol aka *Big Fat Important Movie*: Herself
My Name Is Earl: Herself (1 episode)
  —"I Won't Die with a Little Help from My Friends: Part 2" TV
    episode: Herself

Wetten, dass..?: Herself
—"Wetten, dass..? aus Erfurt" TV episode: Herself
Pop Fiction: Herself (1 episode)
—TV episode #1.1: Herself

Documentary:

Paris, Not France [Actress]
My Longest Day [thanks]
50 Greatest Families (TV): The Hilton Family

Executive Producer:

Paris Hilton's My New BFF Reunion Special (TV)
Paris Hilton's BFF Thanksgiving Special (TV)
Paris Hilton's My New BFF (7 episodes, 2008)
The Hottie & the Nottie

Writer:

Paris Hilton's My New BFF (7 episodes, 2008)

Reality TV/Awards Shows/Special Appearances:

Paris Hilton's My New BFF
   "Welcome to the Dollhouse" (September 30, 2008): Herself
   "24 Hour Party Challenge" (October 7, 2008): Herself
   "Sayonara!" (October 14, 2008): Herself
   "Who's the Fakest?" (October 21, 2008): Herself
   "You Gotta Have Class" (October 28, 2008): Herself
   "Vegas, Baby!" (November 4, 2008): Herself
   "My Kind of People" (November 11, 2008)
   "Keep Your Frenemies Closer" (November 18, 2008)
   "Our Friendship Is Over" (November 25, 2008): Herself
Exclusiv—Das Star-Magazin: Herself (1 episode, 2008)
   —TV episode dated December 21, 2008: Herself
Buenafuente: Herself (1 episode, 2008)
   —TV episode dated December 10, 2008: Herself

The Victoria's Secret Fashion Show (TV): Herself
2008 American Music Awards (TV): Herself—Presenter
Up Close with Carrie Keagan: Herself (3 episodes, 2008)
   —TV episode dated November 6, 2008: Herself
   —TV episode dated May 1, 2008: Herself
   —TV episode dated February 8, 2008: Herself
Paris Hilton Gets Presidential with Martin Sheen (Video): Herself
Backstage Exclusive at the National Television Awards (TV): Herself
The National Television Awards 2008 (TV): Herself—Presenter
MTV Video Music Awards 2008 (TV): Herself
Paris Hilton Responds to McCain Ad (Video): Herself

Thanks:

My Longest Day (thanks)

2009

Acting:

Supernatural: Leshii (1 episode, 2009)
   —"Fallen Idols" TV episode: Leshii
Rex (TV): Paris

Documentary:

Clubland: Herself
Sundance Skippy [Actress]

Executive Producer:

Paris Hilton's My New BFF: Season 2
Paris Hilton's British Best Friend TV series

Writer:

Paris Hilton's My New BFF: Season 2
Paris Hilton's British Best Friend TV series

Reality TV/Awards Shows/Special Appearances:

Paris Hilton's British Best Friend
  Episode #1.1 (January 29, 2009): Herself
  Episode #1.2 (February 5, 2009): Herself
  Episode #1.3 (February 12, 2009): Herself
  Episode #1.4 (February 19, 2009): Herself
  Episode #1.5 (February 26, 2009): Herself
  Episode #1.6 (March 5, 2009): Herself
  Episode #1.7 (March 12, 2009): Herself, Writer
  Episode #1.8 (March 19, 2009): Herself, Writer

Paris Hilton's My New BFF: Season 2
  Episode 201 "No More Hungry Tigers" Posted June 2, 2009
  Episode 202 "Sisters Before Misters" Posted June 9, 2009
  Episode 203 "What's on the Inside and the Outside Counts"
    Posted June 16, 2009
  Episode 204 "Can You Hang With My Friends?" Posted June 23,
    2009
  Episode 205 "Learn From Your Mistakes" Posted June 30, 2009
  Episode 206 "Have My Back" Posted July 7, 2009
  Episode 207 "Must Have Good Taste" Posted July 14, 2009
  Episode 208 "Must Have A Thick Skin" Posted July 21, 2009
  Episode 209 "Where Do You Come From?" Posted July 28, 2009
  Episode 210 "Do You Really Know Me?" Posted August 4, 2009

A-List Awards (TV): Herself
2009 MTV Movie Awards (TV): Herself
I Get That a Lot (TV): Herself
Bondi Rescue: Herself (1 episode, 2009)
  —TV episode #5.2: Herself
Ant & Dec's Saturday Night Takeaway: Herself—Guest Announcer
    (1 episode, 2009)
  —TV episode #9.1: Herself—Guest Announcer
The 51st Annual Grammy Awards (TV): Herself
Loose Women: Herself (1 episode, 2009)
  —TV episode #13.99: Herself
The 35th Annual People's Choice Awards (TV): Herself
Crystal Audigier, tel père telle fille TV series: Herself

Fox Reality Really Awards (TV): Herself
Kathy Griffin: My Life on the D-List: Herself (1 episode, 2009)
   —"Paris Is My New BFF" TV episode: Herself
Denise Richards: It's Complicated: Herself (1 episode, 2009)
   —"Denise Does Slamdance" TV episode: Herself

Thanks:

The Chronicles of Holly-Weird (special thanks)

2010

Acting:

The Other Guys: Jane
Caiga quien caiga: Herself (1 episode, 2010)
   —TV episode dated June 6, 2010: Herself
With Great Power: The Stan Lee Story [Actress]

Documentary:

Teenage Paparazzo: Herself
Talk Show Appearances/News Shows (partial list)
The Barbara Walters Special [Self]
The 10 Most Fascinating People of 2004 TV episode [Actress]
Celebrities Uncensored
   —TV episode #2.6 (2004): Herself
   —TV episode #2.3 (2004): Herself
   —TV episode #1.15 (2003): Herself
   —TV episode #1.14 (2003): Herself
   —TV episode #1.8 (2003): Herself
Corazón de . . .
   —TV episode dated November 16, 2006: Herself
   —TV episode dated November 23, 2005: Herself
   —TV episode dated October 20, 2005: Herself
   —TV episode dated October 18, 2005: Herself
   —TV episode dated October 3, 2005: Herself
   —TV episode dated January 10, 2007: Herself

—TV episode dated November 22, 2005: Herself
—TV episode dated November 16, 2005: Herself
—TV episode dated November 10, 2005: Herself
Da Ali G Show [Self]
—"Law" (2003) TV episode [Actress]
Die Johannes B. Kerner Show [Self]
—TV episode dated May 19, 2005 [Actress]
Dogg After Dark: Herself (2 episodes, 2009)
—TV episode #1.1 (2009): Herself
—TV episode #1.3 (2009): Herself
Ellen: The Ellen DeGeneres Show: Herself (11 episodes, 2004–9)
—TV episode dated December 16, 2009: Herself
—TV episode dated March 9, 2009: Herself
—TV episode dated November 12, 2008: Herself
—TV episode dated November 3, 2008: Herself
—TV episode dated October 7, 2008: Herself
—TV episode dated February 8, 2008: Herself
—TV episode dated November 28, 2007: Herself
—TV episode dated May 1, 2006: Herself
—TV episode dated May 6, 2005: Herself
—TV episode dated January 26, 2005: Herself
—TV episode dated August14, 2004: Herself
Entertainment Tonight: Herself (21 episodes, 2007–8)
—TV episode dated October 8, 2008: Herself
—TV episode dated September 15, 2008: Herself
—TV episode dated September 12, 2008: Herself
—TV episode dated August 27, 2008: Herself
—TV episode dated August 7, 2008: Herself
—TV episode dated August 6, 2008: Herself
—TV episode dated May 20, 2008: Herself
—TV episode dated April 23, 2008: Herself
—TV episode dated February 8, 2008: Herself
—TV episode dated February 5, 2008: Herself
—TV episode dated January 2, 2008: Herself
—TV episode dated December 27, 2007: Herself
—TV episode dated December 12, 2007: Herself
—TV episode dated September 27, 2007: Herself

—TV episode dated September 11, 2007: Herself
—TV episode dated August 28, 2007: Herself
—TV episode dated August 17, 2007: Herself
—TV episode dated August 16, 2007: Herself
—TV episode dated August 10, 2007: Herself
—TV episode dated July 31, 2007: Herself
—TV episode dated July 30, 2007: Herself
Extra: Herself (2 episodes, 2005–7)
—TV episode dated July 30, 2007: Herself
—TV episode dated April 27, 2005: Herself
Fashion File [Self]
—"Mercedes-Benz Fashion Week" TV episode [Actress]
Fashion in Focus [Self]
—"New Kids on the Block: Part 2" (2004) TV episode [Actress]
Good Day Live [Self]
—TV episode dated January 25, 2005 [Actress]
Good Morning America [Self]
—TV episode dated May 31, 2005 [Actress]
In the Cutz [Self] aka *In the Mix*—USA (original title)
—"Elite Models Strut and Playboy Bunnies Play Poker" (2006)
   TV episode [Actress]
Jimmy Kimmel Live!: Herself (2 episodes, 2009)
—TV episode dated October 30, 2009: Herself
—TV episode dated June 12, 2009: Herself
Larry King Live: Herself (1 episode, 2007)
—"Paris Hilton" TV episode: Herself
The Late Late Show with Craig Ferguson: Herself (4 episodes,
   2008–9)
   TV episode #6.71 (2009): Herself
   TV episode #5.191 (2009): Herself
   TV episode #5.45 (2009): Herself
   TV episode #5.61 (2008): Herself
Late Night with Conan O'Brien [Self]
—TV episode dated September 10, 2004 (2004) [Actress]
Late Show with David Letterman
   Episode #12.98 (February 11, 2005): Herself—Guest
   Episode dated April 28, 2005: Herself

Episode dated June 12, 2006: Herself

Episode #15.14 (September 28, 2007): Herself—Guest

Episode #15.57 (February 1, 2008): Herself—Guest

Episode #15.112 (May 8, 2008): Herself—Guest

Episode #16.13 (September 25, 2008): Herself—Guest

Episode #16.35 (November 3, 2008): Herself—Guest

Episode #16.152 (June 5, 2009): Herself—Guest

Episode #17.83 (February 3, 2010): Herself—Top Ten List Presenter

Le grand journal de Canal+ [Self]

—TV episode dated May 13, 2005 [Actress]

Live from Studio Five: Herself (1 episode, 2009)

—TV episode #1.33 (2009): Herself

Live with Regis [Self] aka *Live with Regis and Kathie Lee* aka *Live with Regis & Kelly*

—TV episode dated April 29, 2005 [Actress]

NBC Nightly News [Self]

—TV episode dated May 26, 2005 [Actress]

Queer Edge with Jack E. Jett [Self]

—TV episode #1.20 (2005) [Actress]

Street Customs: Herself (1 episode, 2009)

—"Escalade & Smart Car" (2009) TV episode: Herself

Taff (German talk show)[Self]

—TV episode dated January 3, 2007 [Actress]

—TV episode dated December 29, 2006 [Actress]

—TV episode dated December 28, 2006 [Actress]

—TV episode dated December 22, 2006 [Actress]

This Morning [Self]

—TV episode dated May 26, 2005 [Actress]

Tinseltown TV [Self]

—TV episode dated September 13, 2003 [Actress]

The Tonight Show with Conan O'Brien: Herself (1 episode, 2009)

—TV episode #1.10 (2009): Herself

The Tonight Show with Jay Leno [Self]

—TV episode dated June 15, 2005 [Actress]

—TV episode #17.27 (n.d.) [Actress]

The Tony Danza Show [Self]

—TV episode dated May 11, 2005 [Actress]

—TV episode #1.4 (2004) [Actress]

Total Request Live: Herself

—TV episode dated May 5, 2005: Herself

—TV episode dated September 9, 2004: Herself

The Wendy Williams Show: Herself (1 episode, 2009)

—TV episode dated November 4, 2009: Herself

Wiener Opernball [Self]

—TV episode dated February 15, 2007 [Actress]

The View [Self]

—TV episode dated June 15, 2006 [Actress]

—TV episode dated May 5, 2005 [Actress]

Awards

2004

Nominated

    1. Teen Choice Award Choice TV Personality: Female Choice Reality/Variety TV Star—Female for *The Simple Life* (2003)

    2. Teen Choice Award Choice TV Personality

2005

Nominated

    1. Teen Choice Award Choice Crossover Artist

    2. Teen Choice Award Choice Movie Breakout Performance—Female for *House of Wax* (2005)

    3. Teen Choice Award Choice TV Personality: Female

    4. X-Rated Critics' Organization, USA XRCO Award Mainstream Adult Media Favorite

Won

Teen Choice Award Choice Movie Scream Scene for *House of Wax* (2005)

2006

Nominated

    1. MTV Movie Award, Best Frightened Performance for *House of Wax* (2005)

2. Razzie Award Most Tiresome Tabloid Targets Paris Hilton and . . . Who-EVER!
3. Teen Choice Award TV—Choice Reality Star (Female) for *The Simple Life* (2003)

Won

Razzie Award, Worst Supporting Actress for *House of Wax* (2005)

2007

Nominated

Teen Choice Award Choice TV: Female Reality/Variety Star for *The Simple Life* (2003)

2009

Won

Razzie Awards for
1. Worst Actress for *The Hottie and the Nottie* (2008)
2. Worst Screen Couple for *The Hottie and the Nottie* (2008) shared with Christine Lakin and Joel Moore
3. Worst Supporting Actress for *Repo! The Genetic Opera* (2008)

Nominated

Teen Choice Award, Choice TV Female Reality/Variety Star for *Paris Hilton's My New BFF* (2008)

2010

Won

Razzie Award Worst Actress of the Decade for *The Hottie and the Nottie* (2008)

Nominated for five "achievements," "winner" of four Razzies; also for *House of Wax* (2005) and *Repo! The Genetic Opera* (2008)

Other Works

Music:

Album: *Paris*, Heiress, Warner Bros. Records 44138, 2006. Standard edition

"Turn It Up" 3:12
"Fightin' Over Me" 4:01
"Stars Are Blind" 3:56
"I Want You" 3:12
"Jealousy" 3:40
"Heartbeat" 3:43
"Nothing in This World" 3:10
"Screwed" 3:41
"Not Leaving Without You" 3:35
"Turn You On" 3:06
"Do Ya Think I'm Sexy?" 4:34
Special edition
Includes a Bonus DVD containing "Paris—The Music Special"
   (featuring "Making the Album" and "Behind the Scenes" foot-
   age) and Jealousy in the Studio

Singles:

"Stars Are Blind," Heiress, Warner Bros. Records 42967, 2006,
   Billboard Hot Dance Club Play—#18, Billboard Hot 100
"Turn It Up" (Club single only, no music video filmed)—#1, Bill-
   board Dance single sales
"Nothing in This World"—#12 U.S. Billboard Hot Dance Club
   Play; #89, Billboard Pop 100

Music videos:

"Caught Up in the Rapture" by Won-G (2004)
"Don't Let the Men Get You Down" by Fatboy Slim (2004)
"Just Lose It" by Eminem (2004)

Books:

Confessions of an Heiress with Merle Ginsburg (Fireside/Simon &
   Schuster, 2004)
Your Heiress Diary: Confess It All to Me with Merle Ginsburg (Fire-
   side/Simon & Schuster, 2005)

Print ads:

Iceberg jeans (2001)
Guess clothing (2004–5)
Hollywood Prescription lip hydration system (2005)
Devassa beer (2010)

TV commercial:

T-Mobile cell phones (2004)
Carl's Jr. hamburger store chain (2005)
For German TV: GoYellow (2005)
Devassa beer (2010)

Magazine cover photo

Elle (Poland) February 2008
Celebrity Skin (USA) December 2007, vol. 30, iss. 172
Veronica (Netherlands) May 5, 2007, iss. 18
Blender (USA) September 2006, vol. 5, iss. 8
Der Spiegel (Germany) January 9, 2006
Celebrity Sleuth (USA) 2006, iss. 43
Real People (Greece) October 9, 2005, iss. 33
Hitkrant (Netherlands) June 4, 2005, iss. 22
Het Nieuwsblad (Belgium) May 25, 2005
Seventeen (USA) March 2005, vol. 64, iss. 3
Playboy (USA) March 2005, vol. 52, iss. 3
Beau Monde (Netherlands) February 11, 2005, iss. 3
For Men (Greece) 2005, iss. 42
Veronica (Netherlands) September 25, 2004, iss. 39
Celebrity Skin (USA) September 2004, iss. 132
Celebrity Sleuth (USA) August 2004, iss. 33
Télépro (Belgium) June 17, 2004, iss. 2624
Celebrity Sleuth (USA) June 2004, iss. 32
Movieline's Hollywood Life (USA) June 2004, vol. 14, iss. 15
Ice (UK) June 2004, iss. 33
Maxim (USA) April 2004, iss. 76
FHM (USA) March 2004

Elle (USA) March 2004

Beau Monde (Netherlands) February 13, 2004, iss. 3

Zink (USA) February 2004

Ralph (Australia) February 2004

Celebrity Skin (USA) January 2004, vol. 28, iss. 124

Salon City (USA) January 2004

Celebrity Skin (USA) January 2004, vol. 28, iss. 125

Celebrity Sleuth (USA) 2004, iss. 36

Toronto Globe Television (Canada) December 27, 2003

The Star (USA) December 23, 2003

TV Guide (USA) December 6, 2003

Us Weekly (USA) December 1, 2003

Ocean Drive (USA) December 2003

Vegas (USA) December 2003

Toronto Sun Television (Canada) November 30, 2003

New York Vue (USA) November 30, 2003

TV Time (USA) November 30, 2003

New York Post TV Week (USA) November 30, 2003

TV Guide (Canada) November 29, 2003

Steppin' Out (USA) November 26, 2003

Seventeen (USA) October 2003

Radar (USA) 2003, vol. 1, iss. 2

FHM (USA) May 2002

FHM (Australia) February 2002

SELECTED BIBLIOGRAPHY

Books

Hilton, Conrad. *Be My Guest*. Englewood Cliffs, NJ: Prentice Hall, 1957.

Hilton, Paris, with Merle Ginsberg. *Confessions of an Heiress*. New York: Fireside, 2005.

Newkey-Burden, Chas. *Paris Hilton: Life on the Edge*. London: John Blake, 2007.

Oppenheimer, Jerry. *House of Hilton*. New York: Random House, 2006.

Articles

Brown, Laura. "Partners in Crime." *Harper's Bazaar* 3547, June 2007, 134.

Hardy, Rebecca. "So, Mrs. Hilton, Are You Ashamed of Your Daughter?" *Daily Mail* (London), May 23, 2008, 15.

Sales, Nancy Jo. "Hip Hop Debs." *Vanity Fair*, Sept. 2000, 350.

Documentary/Transcripts

"Interview with Paris Hilton," CNN *Larry King Live*, June 27, 2007, transcripts.cnn.com/TRANSCRIPTS/0706/27/lkl.01.html.

Paris, Not France. Directed by Adria Petty. Documentary. New York: MTV, 2008.

Web Sites

www.imdb.com/name/nm0385296. Paris Hilton, Internet Movie Data-Base.

www.parishilton.com. Paris's own Web site, featuring the latest information on her products, projects, and other doings.

www.parishiltononline.net. The number-one online fan resource for all things Paris Hilton.

www.parishiltonsite.net. A tribute to the multitalented icon Paris Hilton.

www.perezhilton.com. Celebrity juice; the go-to source for daily happenings in Hollywood.

INDEX

About the Author

SANDRA GURVIS (www.sgurvis.com) is the author of 16 books and hundreds of magazine articles. Her titles include *Day Trips from Columbus* (3rd ed., 2009); *Careers for Nonconformists* (2000), which was a selection of the Quality Paperback Book Club; *America's Strangest Museums* (1998; 1996); and more. Her books have been featured on *Good Morning America, CBS Up to the Minute,* and *ABC World News Tonight;* in *USA Today* and in other newspapers and magazines; and on television and radio stations across the country. Her newest titles are *Ohio Curiosities* (2007; 2nd ed., 2011), *Management Basics* (2nd ed., 2007), and *Managing the Telecommuting Employee,* with Michael Amigoni (2009). She recently completed her second novel, *Country Club Wives*.